Brothers, Are You Listening?

A Success Guide for the 90's

By
Michael Taylor

"How to create a life filled with Joy, Passion and Success!"

Creation Publishing Group™

Houston, Texas

Copyright© 1994 by Creation Publishing Group
Houston, Texas

Printed in the United States of America

ISBN #0-9641894-0-2
Library of Congress #94-60671

Brothers, Are You Listening?
by Michael Taylor

Published by:
Creation Publishing Group
6355 Westheimer #187
Houston, Texas 77057

All rights reserved. No part of this book may be reproduced in any manner, in whole of in part, in English or in any other language, in hard copy or in electronic media without written permission from the publisher except for brief quotations in books, magazines, or critical reviews.

BROTHERS, ARE YOU LISTENING?

A SUCCESS GUIDE FOR THE 90'S

FORWARD	4
ACKNOWLEDGMENTS	6
PREFACE	7
CHAPTER ONE: The "That's What White People Do" Mentality	9
CHAPTER TWO: Personal Growth: An Investment in Self	31
CHAPTER THREE: Relationships	47
CHAPTER FOUR: Sex and Manhood	63
CHAPTER FIVE: Children	75
CHAPTER SIX: Health and Fitness	87
CHAPTER SEVEN: Success and Wealth	99
CHAPTER EIGHT: God and Spirituality	111
CHAPTER NINE: Purpose	121
CHAPTER TEN: Service	131

FORWARD

TELL IT LIKE IT IS IN

10 EXHILARATING EPISODES

Brothers, are you listening?

Success is ours, make the discovery.

Dispel the old myth and move forward.

Wake-up black men, wake-up, it's nobody elses fault.

Let's make a difference in our lives.

Invest in yourself, you have the power.

Get a career and make a difference.

Wake-up black men, wake-up.

    Journey with Michael Taylor as he tells the situations from early childhood to manhood through ten powerful episodes of memories, experiences and solutions. Developing a positive "mind set" is the key to open the door for success. The stimulating messages in this document are timely wake-up calls for young men who might be struggling with life difficulties and disappointments. This powerful documentary provides a profound view of Taylor's experiences. He begins each chapter with a situation and ends with solutions, recommendations and challenges to his brethren. Never have the messages been told to the brothers as Taylor shares them. His style will surely capture his audience. Allow yourself, take the journey in ten exhilarating episodes with Michael Taylor as he shares with ALL-MEN, ALL-MEN, AND ALL-MEN in a nutshell.

Maxine Hammonds-Smith, Ph.D., CFLE

SUCCESS: THREE COMMON DENOMINATORS
Knowing at an early age
Experiencing a period of hardship
Guiding feelings within

- **It's a Matter of Thinking**, so why don't we make
- **An Investment in Ourselves**, find yourself first, then build a
- **Relationship**, understand the gender "male" and "female" and the situation "sexual" and "sensual".
- **Sex and Manhood** will surely come.

- **Health and Fitness** for the 90s "save lives and live longer", a motto for the brothers.
- **Children**, our future, we are all in it together, 9 months to 90 years, we are family.

- **Success and Wealth**, invest in it, ask questions, answer them and move forward.
- **God and Spirituality**, find that place that works for "you", know the truth about your Spiritual Being.

- **Purpose** for Being, live, let live.

- **Service** to all humankind.

ALL-MEN, ALL-MEN, AND ALL-MEN
Maxine Hammonds-Smith, Ph.D., CFLE

ACKNOWLEDGMENTS

To my Creator:
I understand that what I am is your gift to me, and what I make of myself is my gift to you. I am truly grateful for the gifts and I commit myself to using them in your service. I am eternally grateful for the joy and peace I feel within, Thanks for keeping your promise!

To my Soul-Mate Renee:
Without question you are my gift from God. I put in my request and I received more than I asked for. Your support allows me to do everything I knew I was capable of, and the best part is I get to do it with you. I hope you have a firm grip, because I'm heading for the stars and I want you to be with me. I'm glad you finally "GOT IT"! I Love You!

To my mom:
Thank you for all the wonderful lessons. I was always listening although it may not have seemed like it. I told you I could do this.

To Charles, Mike and Katrina:
My beautiful God given angels. It was because of you that I found strength when I didn't think I had any left. It was the unconditional love that you give, that kept me focused on my dream. I Love You! Daddy said he knew what he was doing didn't he!

To Daniel Platt, Jane Wise, Norris Rogers, Norman Rennalls, Christine Rogers and my real brothers Roy and Sherman:
Thanks for all the financial, emotional and spiritual support. Although it never really looked the way I planned it, I promised you I would make it to the top and live my dreams, so here I am. God bless you all.

And to all the wonderful people who believed in me and helped me make my dream a reality: I could have never made it without you. I love you all!

MICHAEL

PREFACE

Contrary to what you may be seeing in the media, it is my belief that we are entering into the most exciting, eventful and opportunistic time in the history of our world. As we prepare to enter the next millennium, those of us who are willing to be in control of our own destinies will experience a level of success never before seen in the history of the planet.

I believe the windows of opportunity are wide open for us to capitalize on the wealth of knowledge and information that is now available to everyone. The question I pose is "Will you stand on the outside looking in, or will you jump through that window with excitement, courage and enthusiasm?" If you're still reading, you've already jumped; congratulations, you are well on your way to success in the 90's. I'll see you there!

MICHAEL

I tell you the truth, if anyone says to this mountain, 'Go throw yourself into the sea,' and does not doubt in his heart but BELIEVES that what he says will happen, it will be done for him. Therefore I tell you, whatever you ask for in prayer, BELIEVE that you have received it, and it will be yours.

Mark 11:23

THE "THAT'S WHAT WHITE PEOPLE DO" MENTALITY

I was born in Corpus Christi, Texas, October 22, 1960. I have very vivid memories of my childhood. I remember the projects I grew up in and as a child I remember being labeled as poor. There was something about the word poor that I really didn't like. It had a negative connotation then, and to this day I'm uncomfortable using it. It's been said that everything happens for a reason, so the fact that I decided early that I would not wear that label leads me to believe that there is validity to that statement. My earlier experiences of poverty propelled me to reach higher to avoid being labeled. **I simply made a choice to be successful.** It was this commitment I made to myself that has empowered me to reach far past society's expectations of a young black male. At a very young age I took responsibility for my destiny, and it has brought me not only monetary success, but a deep down feeling of joy, fulfillment and gratitude.

All my life I have been fascinated by the stories of successful people. As I've read their stories and had the opportunity to meet some of them, I have come to the conclusion that each success story has three common denominators.
1. *Most successful people somehow knew at a very early age that they were going to be successful.*
2. *In each case, there was a period of hardship and sometimes tragedy.*
3. *Each individual felt as if there was something within that guided them to their success.*

These are the building blocks of success. Of course there are always exceptions to the rules, but I can assure you nine times out of ten you will find these three elements. My story is no different. At the age of eight I knew exactly what I wanted to do when I grew up. As I look back in retrospect I see the path which led me to my ultimate destiny. The reason I wanted to write this book is to share with you some of my own experiences. Hopefully you will see some parallels to your own life and will be able to learn from my mistakes and successes.

As I look back to the beginning of my life I realize that the foundation for my success started with my mom. The lessons I learned from her were invaluable. She is definitely my greatest inspiration. I think we all can remember some of the lessons taught to us by the person responsible for bringing us into this world, and I would like to share with you some of those lessons.

First and foremost, my mom taught me to have an optimistic attitude. She didn't have to verbalize this lesson because she lived her life that way. Like so many moms, she was faced with incredible adversities, yet she took each one and converted it to an opportunity. As a single mother with six children, she was constantly challenged to somehow find a way to provide for her family. Like too many mothers she had to work several jobs to try and keep food on the table. Despite the many obstacles, she found time to provide a smile, a hug and a sense of hope. She wouldn't allow me to concede to a life of poverty. She told me that I was responsible for my success and no one else. "Always remember, things could always be worse," she would say. It was this attitude of gratitude that stuck with me and allowed me to always find the positive things in any situation.

My mom had a wonderful way of explaining things to me. Although she didn't have a college education she is the smartest person I ever met. She could get a point across in a way that would stay with you for a lifetime. I would like to share with you the lesson she taught me about dealing with racism.

I was approximately five years old and I came running into the house angry, upset and confused. A white kid had called me "nigger" and although I didn't know what the word meant at the time, I could tell by the tone of his voice and the context in which he used it, it was definitely not a nice word.

My mother looked at me and asked, "What's wrong with you?" Normally she would have this very supportive look on her face, but when I told her that this kid called me a nigger she gave me a look that I didn't expect. She looked at me with this sort of stoic expression and started to repeat over and over again, "Nigger, Nigger, Nigger." At first she scared the hell out of me. Then I became afraid that my poor mom had lost her marbles. "Nigger Nigger Nigger," she repeated again. By now I was dumbfounded, then she looked at me and asked, "Did that hurt?" Now I knew she had lost it. Then she asked again, this time a little more forcefully, "Did that hurt?"

"No," I answered, by now I was really confused. Then she started to walk around me as if she were performing a visual body search.

Then she asked another confusing question, "Are you bleeding?" What kind of question was that? By now I knew she had snapped. Then she asked again, "Are you bleeding?"

"No," I answered feeling angry and rejected.

Then in her infinite wisdom she explained the reason for her actions. She took me in her arms and gave me the supportive nurturing look that I was accustomed to. She smiled, gave me a kiss, and said "'Nigger' is just a word, no matter who says it or how it's said it can't hurt you. I realize this isn't fair, but you will probably hear that word a million times in your lifetime. But you can't let a simple word keep you from being successful. Always remember what just happened here and that word will not have an effect on you."

What a powerful lesson! To this day I have never had a problem with racial slurs. As she mentioned, it's not fair, but we have to recognize that it's just a word, and words can't hurt us.

Another great lesson I learned from my mom at an early age was self responsibility. As was the case, it was taught to me through an unconventional method and circumstance.

One day a friend and I were sitting on the seawall at the beach, watching some guys surf.

The "That's What White People Do" Mentality

As I sat there I thought about how fun that must be. A part of me knew that I could do that, so I decided I wanted to learn how to surf. I looked at my friend and said "One day I'm going to learn how to surf."

My friend looked at me sort of puzzled and replied, "No you're not!"

"Yes, I am," I said.

"But you can't do that."

"Why not?" I asked.

"Because that's what white people do," he responded.

"So what, I can learn to surf if I want to."

"But they won't let you," he shouted.

"Who won't let me?"

"The white people, that's who."

"You're crazy! I can learn how to surf if I want to."

"I don't believe you will," he said.

"Just watch and see," I replied.

That night I asked my mom if I could learn how to surf. "Boy, you don't even know how to swim. How are you going to learn how to surf?"

"Well, what about when I get bigger?"

"Sure you can learn, but you're going to have to buy your own surfboard because I'm not going to buy one for you."

"So that means no one can keep me from surfing, right?"

"What do you mean?" she asked.

"Well, today my friend and I were arguing about whether I could learn how to surf or not, and he said that the white people wouldn't let me learn how to surf."

She stopped, looked at me for a moment, then gave me that warm supportive smile. She took me in her arms and said "Michael, *there is absolutely nothing you cannot do, only things you choose not to do!* If you choose to learn how to surf, then no one can stop you but yourself. Always remember, no one can make you do anything or keep you from doing anything you want, except you."

Without question this was the greatest lesson I learned from my mom. It is this lesson that has helped me create the life I knew I deserved. I am forever indebted to her.

Thanks Mom, I love you!

Another significant person in my life was my grandfather. Like my mom, he had incredible wisdom. Although he had experienced all the pain and frustration of being black in the early 1900's, he didn't harbor any hatred towards white people. Whenever he and I discussed the abuses and atrocities inflicted upon black people, he would always say that everything was in God's hand and we shouldn't worry. "God has a plan and we should wait to see what he has in store for us," he would say. I remember thinking to myself that God must have been awfully mad at black people to put them through such hell.

I learned some very valuable lessons from my grandfather. Like my mom, he had a way of explaining things that would clarify any questions I had about a particular topic. I remember an incident that taught me to always focus on knowledge as the key to success.

During my early years in school I was extremely studious. At the age of six I was separated from my mom and had to live with my grandparents. My mother told me to stay in school and get good grades and one day I would be able to be with her again. The separation was extremely painful. As a child my mom was the most important person in my life. But because of circumstances beyond her control she was forced to send me away for awhile. So I decided that the way to get back to the woman I loved was by being smart. During my first through sixth grade years I was a straight A student. I actually loved going to school and learning. I had a favorite teacher named Mrs. Bussy who really challenged me and nurtured my love for learning. She designed a board in our classroom to accommodate the stars we would receive if we received a perfect score on our test. I accumulated so many stars that she had to do an extension after my name. I was basically the teachers pet, and without question the most intelligent.

There was a girl in my class named Susan. Susan was a white girl from an affluent part of town. She was my closest competitor. I would usually beat her in every category. One day after a test I remember teasing her that I was smarter than she was. She looked at me then said, "My mom says that white people are smarter than black people, and that black people are really stupid." I was shocked. Although I had proof this wasn't the case by my grades, there was something very painful in those words. I couldn't even respond. After school I approached my grandfather and asked him if what she said was true. I had heard this before, but had never really given it any consideration.

"Grandfather, are white people really smarter than black people?" I asked.

"Who told you that?" he asked.

"This girl at my school".

My grandfather obviously sensed that I was really troubled by this, so he picked me up and explained. "No, white people aren't any smarter than black people; they simply have more information than we do. You see, when black people were first brought over here, it was against their will. At the time white people had better technology and weapons and were able to force black people to do something they really didn't want to do. So when black people first came to this country, they had to learn a whole new way of life in a place that they knew nothing about. Let me give you another way to look at it. Imagine that you had two people about to run a race. Now imagine that both people run at exactly the same speed. So that means when they run the race it will end in a tie. No matter how far they run they will always finish at the same time. But what do you think will happen if one of them had a head start? If they both run at the same speed then the one that gets the head start will win right? Well that's the best way to look at the difference between black people and white people in this country. White people simply have had a head start, that's all. But don't worry because black people are pretty fast, and we're catching up pretty quickly."

The "That's What White People Do" Mentality

I looked at him and could see the wisdom in his eyes. There was a knowingness about him that I was very comfortable with. I smiled and told him that I understood, and I asked "So that means that I'm one of the fast black people since I do so well in school, Huh, grandfather?"

"That's right, Michael, you are definitely one of the fast black people." Now I had a new mission in life, to be one of the fast black people.

I really enjoyed talking to my grandfather; he would share his dreams with me and would always be willing to try and answer the hundreds of questions I would ask.

One day I walked over to him while he and a friend were playing dominoes. He was extremely passionate about the game. He and his best friend Mr. Pick would spend hours slamming dominoes and talking about life. I would usually just sit there and listen, but this time I had something really important to say. I interrupted his game and said "Grandfather, when I grow up I'm going to be a millionaire."

"And how do you plan on doing that?" he asked.

"I'm going to own my own company," I replied.

"Well that's great, so if that's what you want to do when you grow up, let me give you the secrets to being rich. There are really only two secrets you need to know in order to be rich. I promise that if you remember these two things there is nothing you can't accomplish. Are you listening?"

"Yes, grandfather."

"Well, the first thing you have to do is learn to think like the white man. Now that doesn't mean you are supposed to try and be something you aren't. That simply means you have to think like a person that's rich. Since the white man is the one with all the money, you have to think the way he does. You see, the only difference between people with money and the people without money is the way that they think. *If you train your mind to think rich thoughts, then you can be rich.* But if you train your mind to have poor thoughts, then you'll be poor. Since the white man has always had all the money, he automatically thinks rich thoughts. And since blacks haven't really made a lot of money yet, most of them think poor thoughts. Always think like the person who has all the money.

"The second thing you need to do is *learn how to listen*. Now that doesn't mean listening to these fools walking around here that don't have anything. You have to listen to the people that have what you want. That means reading their stories and learning how they got rich. If you learn how to listen, then most people will be glad to share their stories with you. Once you've listened, then take the information and make it work for you. That way you've learned from other people's mistakes, and can avoid doing the same thing. I promise if you learn to do those two things, there is absolutely nothing you can't accomplish."

I smiled and let those words of wisdom sink deep within my soul. A part of me knew that these were the keys to my success. I made a commitment to incorporate these ideas into my everyday life.

Across the street from where I lived was a wooded area. Within this wooded area I created a special hideaway for myself. Most of my childhood was pretty isolated, I spent the majority of my time alone. But within the confines of this wooded place I created my own place of power and recognition. I created a mock office which was my home away from home. No one ever knew of my special place. I would go there and spend hours on end negotiating mock business deals with fictitious businessmen. This was my world, and within this space there was no limitation to what I could do or be. At the age of twelve I was reading business publications and following my grandfather's advice of thinking like rich people. I would pretend to be this incredibly powerful businessman, and I would negotiate million dollar deals in oil and real estate. I loved this place. While I was there, I was in control, I dictated what went on and I loved feeling so powerful. At the time it was really all I had. My guardians neglected me and I really hated being separated from my mom, so I created my own safe little world where there was some sense of stability in my life.

In this place I would read stories of successful people and how they created their wealth. I literally spent hundreds of hours reading and thinking how to create the same wealth for myself.

After approximately seven years I was reunited with my mom. I was really glad to be leaving, but a part of me really missed my make-believe office in the woods. But I had been given the keys to living my dreams, now I was getting old enough to actually start creating some wealth of my own. At the age of thirteen I got my first job sweeping floors at a motorcycle shop. At fifteen I was a head stocker for a grocery store and would get up at 5 o'clock in the morning to unload the trucks then go to school at 8 o'clock. At seventeen I was driving a soft drink truck delivering soda. Then at nineteen I started working for a major building supply retailer, for whom I worked for almost ten years. Approximately four years ago I left that job to chase my dream of owning my own company and after three and a half years of rejections, humiliation and sacrifice I finally secured funding to get my organization off the ground. I am now currently living my dream, and I'm sure that the future is very bright for me and my organization.

That is a very brief overview of my life. The point that I'm trying to make is that we create certain beliefs during our childhood that sets the stage for the rest of our lives. During the last few years I've done an incredible amount of research in the areas of metaphysics, physics, psychology and philosophy and I have come to the conclusion that our thoughts really do shape our reality. I don't claim to have all the answers, and for the most part I'll be sharing my opinions and beliefs. It will be up to you to decide what you can use and what you can't. My only request is that you take some time and remain open-minded. Read through the chapters and stories and notice if there are any similarities in your own life. If so use the information provided to make a change in your own life.

Remember, I'm just a regular person just like you that wants to share my experiences. My

The "That's What White People Do" Mentality

hope is that you will gain something that will make your life a little better and hopefully you will be able to pass it on.

So are you ready to be empowered? Are you willing to keep an open mind and be receptive to any message that might be in this book for you? Are you committed to success in the 90's? If so then let's get busy!

Let's take a moment and think about the power of belief. Remember when you were a kid and you believed in Santa Clause, or maybe the Easter Bunny. Maybe you won't admit to that, but how about when you believed in monsters. Remember sitting up thinking that there was a monster in your closet, and you were scared to death. Although these things weren't real, our belief in them created fear, happiness, sadness and excitement. As children we were extremely open-minded and it was easy for us to believe almost anything. As we become older we get a little more skeptical and not as gullible, and it's almost impossible to get us to believe anything we can't prove or quantify.

The point is that as long as it's real in our minds, then our bodies respond with appropriate actions and reactions. Here's another example. Imagine that you are out of town and you get a call and someone says that your mom has died. If you believe it then you will more than likely experience pain and sorrow. You may become sad and begin to cry or you may simply become depressed. But everything is currently taking place in your mind. So what if you went home and found out that it wasn't true. Imagine that it was a case of mistaken identity and your mom was fine, now what would you experience? Happiness, joy, whatever. The point is, at the time you believed your mom was dead your entire being shifted into a response that was appropriate to your feelings and belief about death. Your belief in her death created the experience of death within your mind. I'm not going to try and explain the entire process, I simply want to give you a foundation to build on.

Our beliefs about ourselves and the world around us have a lot to do with the experiences we create in our lives. If you've ever studied the great spiritual masters you will find that most of their teachings were based on belief or faith. It's been defined as "Evidence of things unseen." (As quoted from Howard Caesar, a Unity minister in Houston.) It is the beliefs that we hold in our minds that create the world around us. There is a metaphysical saying, "Thoughts held in mind creates likes of it's kind." There is definitely a lot of validity to that statement. So without a lot of technical jargon, let's discuss the origin or our beliefs.

From the moment we're born we are bombarded with images and messages. This is the time when we start creating our main core beliefs about ourselves. Of course our parents are our main source of information, and they normally provide us with either positive or negative beliefs about ourselves.

A perfect analogy of how this process works is the personal computer. When you purchase a computer there is absolutely no information in it. It's basically an empty box of wires and chips. Once you decide what you want your computer to do you have the option to add different programs. You can also add megs of memory and other items, but since I'm making a simple analogy I won't bore you with technicalities. The point that I want to make is the computer has a device that's called the hard drive. The hard drive is located within the body of the computer and in most cases it will not be removed. It stores your main programs on what's called a hard disk. The information that is stored on this hard disk is semi-permanent. As I mentioned, once you purchase your computer you have the option as to what information you want programed on that hard disk. In addition to the hard disk there are floppy disk. A floppy disk contains information that can be fed into the computer from the outside. It contains information that you insert into the computer, and the computer takes that information, then processes it and responds.

I want you to remember that the hard disk is the internal disk and the floppy disk is the external disk. I will be referring back to this analogy throughout the book.

So let's use an example of how this process works. Let's imagine that we have two children born at the same time in the same hospital. When these babies are born there minds are basically blank (Just like the new computer). Baby #1 comes into a family that is nurturing and loving. When the parents take her home, they are constantly cuddling her and providing her with love and affection. They tell baby #1 how beautiful she is and how happy they are that she was born. They give her positive affirmations and shower her with compliments.

Baby #2 on the other hand has parents that are constantly telling her how stupid she is. All she hears is how her parents wish she had never been born. She is constantly yelled at and neglected. They also tell her how ugly she is.

What is actually taking place the first three years of these children's lives is, their parents are loading their hard disk with information or beliefs about themselves. This information becomes semi-permanent on that child's hard disk. This information will be the foundation for how that child feels about themselves for the rest of their lives or until that child decides to change that information. It is the basis for a person's self esteem.

So based on this scenario what type of beliefs do you think each child will have about themselves?

So now that we know what type of information is stored on their hard disk. Let's talk about inserting some information on a floppy disk.

Let's imagine that information was "I really think you're beautiful." Now remember we're putting in information from an external disk. When we do that, the computer has to take that external information, then process it before it can respond. If the computer has the same information stored on the hard disk it can process it, then respond in the appropriate manner. If it doesn't have that information, it will reject the outside information.

When baby #1 receives the information, she takes it, processes it, finds that information on her hard disk, then responds with an accepting "Thank you." On the other hand, baby #2 receives the information but when she tries to process it, her mind can't find it on her hard drive. So she rejects that information and responds with something like "No you don't!", and turns away.

No matter how hard you try you can not get baby #2 to accept that information. What has happened is baby #2 has created a belief that no one loves her. And because of this belief she will never be able to accept love from anyone unless she goes in and erases the negative beliefs and replaces them with positive beliefs.

Take a moment and think about your childhood. Ask yourself what are some of the beliefs you created about yourself that may need to be changed. As simplistic as it sounds, that's exactly the way our minds work. We form beliefs based on the information we have stored on our hard disk. The first few years of life are the most critical. That's when we are programming our minds.

As I mentioned, the information that is stored on our hard disk is *semi*-permanent. That means it can be changed. But it takes a willing participant with a commitment to themselves to make the changes. This process can be emotionally painful. But it is my belief that there are no shortcuts. If you really want to replace the old beliefs with new beliefs, you have to be willing to start at the beginning. That means identifying the origin of the beliefs and being able to erase all the old information and replace it with new information. I will go into more detail in the next chapter.

So now that you have a better understanding of beliefs and how they are formed, let's discuss some of the core beliefs that I incorporated that has allowed me to live my dreams.

1. WORDS CAN'T HURT YOU!

Living in a society that has not yet learned to deal with it's diversity makes this extremely important to remember and adhere to. People always react based on their core beliefs. Because of the negative images that have been promoted about black men a lot of people have created negative beliefs. This is why it's so important that the media take responsibility for the way we are portrayed. The media without question does an irresponsible job of portraying the reality of most black men. But we have to remember that we are responsible for our own actions. We have to become committed to dealing with our own problems, therefore we could eliminate the negative stories that the media loves to showcase. Since the focus of this book is success, I would like to suggest that whenever you're confronted with racial slurs, ask yourself who's responsible for you being angry? The truth is no one can make you angry but you. So ask yourself if there is an alternative to losing your cool. I promise you there is. Remember the lesson my mom taught me. Just visualize your mom or mine putting you through the process I went through. After awhile it will become funny. I promise if you would have been there you would not have a problem with words hurting you. Remember the old saying " Sticks and stones may break my bones but names will never hurt me."

2. THERE IS NOTHING YOU CANNOT DO, ONLY THINGS YOU CHOOSE NOT TO DO!

Remember the power of belief. As a human being you have the power within you to do anything that has ever been accomplished by another human being. I don't care if it's losing a hundred pounds, making a million dollars or curing yourself of a terminal illness, you have the capacity to do anything. The only thing you need to do is believe that you can. Some of you may struggle with this a little so let me give you some proof. If I can work my way up the corporate ladder, earn fifty thousand dollars a year and buy my first home at the age of twenty three, then lose absolutely everything through divorce, bankruptcy and foreclosure, then pick myself back up and start my own company, write this book and live my dreams with only an eleventh grade education, don't you think you could also? I know you can, the only difference between me and you is I simply believed that I could do it.

I realize the media is constantly creating the belief in most people's mind that the world is a terrible place, and we're entering into the last days before the end. But I promise you that is a bunch of garbage. If you choose to accept that belief then guess what you will experience in your life? There has never been a better time to be alive on this planet than right now. It's up to you to take advantage of all the opportunities available today. No one is responsible for your success except you.

Speaking of beliefs, have you heard the term paradigm shift? Rather than try to give a definition, let me give you an example. Not too long ago the "Experts" said it was physically impossible for a human being to run a four minute mile. They were convinced that the human body could not stand up to what they thought was an incredible strain on the human anatomy. Then one day this guy named Banister decided he didn't believe what the experts had said. He believed that he could and would break the four minute mile. Guess what? He broke the four minute mile! But that's only half the story: Within just a few weeks more than ten other people broke the same barrier. So what happened? Mr. Banister believed that he could do it and once he did it more people simply believed they could do it also. What Mr. Banister did was create a paradigm shift.

Let's talk about a paradigm shift that's closer to home. Remember when society said black people couldn't direct movies? Then Spike Lee decided that he could, and he directed *"She's Gotta Have It."* It was a huge hit. (He may not have been the first, but he definitely set the precedent) But the point is: Did you know that within two years there were 19 other black directors? What happened? A simple shift in belief systems. I believe the next major paradigm shift will be "Black Businesses." I personally want to be the first self-made black billionaire. We'll see what happens.

You have to know that you can do anything you set your mind to. All you have to do is believe that you can.

3. YOU HAVE TO LEARN TO THINK LIKE THE WHITE MAN!

This we can change a bit. At the time there weren't nearly as many successful black people as there are today, so let's change that to, *"You have to learn to think like anyone who has money or the things you want!"*

Before you can start thinking like someone who has what you want, you need to decide what it is. The reason most people don't live their dreams is because they have no idea what their dreams are. So my first suggestion is that you decide exactly what it is that you really

The "That's What White People Do" Mentality

want. Make sure that it's something that's quantifiable. As a matter of fact, why don't you take a moment and write down ten things that you want or want to accomplish.

1. _____

2. _____

3. _____

4. _____

5. _____

6. _____

7. _____

8. _____

9. _____

10. _____

If you couldn't come up with ten things, try five, but I think you should at least have ten. I have several lists in which I've written down 100!! If you didn't write any down, ask yourself why not. *Putting things down on paper is the first step to living your dreams.* When you write things down, it's like making a commitment to yourself that you really are serious. It's the first step of action. I hope you take it. I recommend that you start keeping a journal. Get into the habit of writing down ideas and thoughts that flow through your mind. The more you do this the easier and more fun it gets. Most people will not discipline themselves to take this first step. Then they wonder why they don't have the things they want in their lives.

Once you decide what you really want, start thinking like a person that already has those things. If you want to be a millionaire, you've got to think like one. If you want to be a great public speaker then you've got to think and speak like one. It takes rigor and discipline but for the few dedicated people that put forth the effort, they will reap the fruits of their labor.

Another extremely important element of creating success and living your dreams is visualization. You may not believe it, but, trust me, it works. You need to make visual images in your mind of the things you want and the things you want to do. If you don't believe visualization works, ask former Chicago Bear running back Walter Payton; He attributed a lot of his success to simply seeing himself make touchdowns in his mind before the games. Soul singer Keith Sweat said that he would visualize being on stage in front of hundreds of fans before he even signed his recording contract.

Once I decided to write this book, I would visualize myself at book signings and on talkshows. I would tell my friends how good I was going to look on the Oprah Winfrey show. I would go into the bookstore and visualize my book on the shelf next to my favorite authors. One day I even moved some books over and said, "This is where my books are going to be located." It is a very powerful process, once you choose to believe that it works. In case you need a little assistance, I highly recommend that you purchase *Creative Visualization* by Shakti Gawain. It will assist you in learning how to visualize. It's one of my favorites.

4. YOU HAVE TO LEARN TO LISTEN!

Listening means more than hearing. Listening means receiving information, processing it and then acting on it. Whenever I go to a seminar or workshop, I make sure that I am completely focused on what the speaker is saying. Although I may not agree with everything that's being said, I at least remain open-minded enough to give myself the opportunity to receive the message or lesson. It amazes me to listen to people in the audience at these seminars who are actually arguing that the speaker doesn't know what they're talking about. They automatically create judgments and assessments about the speaker, and ultimately they don't "hear" the message. What a waste! If you choose to go, please choose to listen.

Of course, listening also means reading other peoples stories. This is a must! Not only does reading give you information, but it exercises your brain. Whatever you decide you want to accomplish, read the stories of people that have already done what you want to do. It will condition your thought processes to think like that person. It will also create the belief in your mind that you can do the same thing.

I want to emphasize the fact that you have to be careful who you're listening to. If you're listening to people who always have nothing but negative things to say, then you will eventually start thinking negative thoughts. Les Brown, the great motivational speaker, calls people that think negative thoughts all the time "Toxic People." I think that is a very appropriate title. Even if you are a positive person and think positive thoughts, if you hang around negative people enough, eventually you will become toxic. All those negative thoughts take over your belief systems and pretty soon you're intoxicated with negativity. So make sure you're listening to positive uplifting messages.

So let's summarize the four core beliefs that will propel you to live your dreams.
1. *Words Can't Hurt You!*
2. *There Is Nothing You Cannot Do Only Things You Choose Not To Do!*
3. *You Have To Learn To Think Like People That Have What You Want!*
4. *You Have To Learn To Listen!*

Make a commitment to yourself to go over these on a regular basis. Go to a mirror and affirm to yourself, "Words can't hurt me, and I don't care what other people think about me.

Only I am responsible for my success and I now choose to create a life filled with joy, love and passion. I choose to fill my mind with positive empowering thoughts, and I remove all negative thoughts from my consciousness. I commit myself to gaining the knowledge necessary to live my dreams and I am at peace." Remember the power of belief. If you commit yourself to saying that on a daily basis, soon your mind will start believing it, and you will start seeing a shift in your whole mentality. Consistency and belief work hand in hand. Repetition is the mother of skill. Get committed and start believing.

So now you've received Michael Taylor's secrets of success. Actually they aren't mine. They've been passed down for hundreds of years; I simply believe that they work. Now let's take a look at some of the limiting beliefs that have been passed down throughout society for the last few hundred years.

1. BLACK MEN ARE AN ENDANGERED SPECIES!

I hope you don't believe this. This is the most ludicrous, unsubstantiated myth that I have ever heard. The sad part is some of us actually believe it. I was in a restaurant one day and I happened to over hear a couple of obviously well educated brothers talking about our extinction. These brothers were actually saying things like, "I think brothers will be extinct by the year 2000, if not, then we will probably all be in jail." I am very serious. This was an actual conversation. I walked over to their table and asked, "You brothers really don't believe we're going to be extinct by the year 2000, do you? Please tell me that you're just joking." One of the brothers looked up at me and said, "Where have you been my brother? Haven't you seen the news? At the rate that we're killing each other, there won't be any of us left in ten years." I immediately knew what his beliefs about black men were, and I knew trying to convince him otherwise would have been futile. So I looked him straight in the eye and said "Don't believe the hype, my brother, don't believe the hype." He looked at me sort of puzzled and as I walked away, I could only pray that my brothers wouldn't give up.

So let's set the record straight: We are not an endangered species, and we are not on the verge of extinction. As a matter of fact we're doing quite well, thank you very much. Obviously we have a few problems we need to resolve, but it's nothing we can't handle. The only thing that has been missing from us is urgency. As soon as we decide to put some urgency in addressing our problems, they will go away. As a matter of fact I believe we have made a shift in this area and you are about to see some incredible results. Take a moment and think about what we started out with. Zilch, Nada, Nothing! Remember what my grandfather said about black people being fast? He was right, We're catching up extremely fast, and it's now time for us to take responsibility for our own problems. After you finish reading this book, you'll believe what I'm saying, I promise.

I realize the media has a large majority of people believing this is true. We are constantly bombarded with the statistic that one out of every four blacks are in prison, and there are more blacks in prison than in college. So ask yourself what about the other three. I realize that one brother in jail is too many, but three out of four are pretty darn good odds. Especially if you take into consideration the incredible obstacles and adversities that we have to face on a daily basis.

You have to understand that statistics can be construed to always support a belief. If you have a firm belief about something, then you will go out to create the evidence that supports that belief. For example if you believe that blacks are an endangered species you could easily use the one out of four statistic to support your belief. On the other hand since I know blacks are not an endangered species I can create the evidence that three out of four are doing fine. Now the question becomes who's right. In reality we're both right based on our beliefs. Why do you think we have wars? Because people take a position of being right about their beliefs. In each person's mind they think or believe that they're right. That is the source of all pain and suffering. People simply want to be right about their beliefs and they become close minded to any other way of seeing things.

So rest assured that we are not an endangered species and this is the decade that we have been waiting for. For the first time in our history, we are being recognized for the incredible accomplishments and contributions we've made to this country, and we must continue to focus forward to where we are headed instead of where we have been.

2. THE WHITE MAN IS HOLDING US BACK!

This one won't be as easy to swallow. This is the most powerful of the erroneous beliefs that we hold on to as a race of people. I want you to realize that I am not denying nor minimizing the abuse or injustices inflicted on us as a race of people. I am not saying that everything is fine and there aren't any obstacles and problems. But I want you to stop and just remain open-minded to the next question I'm about to ask you. Remove all negative beliefs from your mind before you answer. Are you ready? Then here's the question:

Who the hell is this guy anyway?
What does he look like?
Can you touch him?
How tall is he?
Does he follow you around, and put his arms around you to
   keep you from living your dreams?
Does he stand in front of the bookstore to keep you from entering?

Now I want you to notice what thoughts and feelings you just went through. Some of you may have agreed with me and supported this belief. Some of you may be rolling on the floor with laughter because you realize the absurdity in this belief. Some of you are probably very angry and are considering whether you want to continue reading or not, and some of you aren't reading anymore because you threw the book across the room and called me a sellout.

So now ask yourself what caused all the different reactions? The answer is very simple, Your core beliefs. Remember the analogy of the computer? When I entered the information

The "That's What White People Do" Mentality

on the floppy disk called "The white man is holding us back," your computer processed that information based on what was on your hard drive. Then you responded based on that information. You may not admit it but it does make sense, doesn't it? Come on move that male ego out of the way and say, "This guy is pretty sharp!"

So let's be serious, if you can't touch it, see it or smell it, it simply isn't real. I don't care how you try to rationalize it, this white man is simply a figment of our imagination. He can only exist in our minds; he isn't real. It is a belief that we have created that is very detrimental to our thought systems. If you don't get anything else out of this book, please get this. As I mentioned I am not saying things are perfect; my question is: "So What Now What?" In comparison to our brothers thirty years ago, we've got it pretty darn easy. We must be willing to remove this limiting belief so we can move to the next millennium without unnecessary baggage. Besides, I'm living proof that with a lot of faith and a commitment to your dream, you can do anything you set your mind to. Please remove this conversation from your consciousness. It will sabotage your dreams.

I would like for you to take a moment and ask yourself when was the last time you had a "Black Pity Party" with some of your friends. You know what I'm talking about don't you? The party goes something like this;

Brother #1: Man it's so hard being black in this country. A brother doesn't stand a chance here.

Brother #2: You ain't lying, man. The White Man keeps holding us back.

Brother #3: Not only that now we've got all these Orientals taking our jobs.

Brother #1: I could have really done a lot with my life if I didn't have this strike against me. If people weren't so prejudiced against black people, I know I could have done a lot more in my life.

Brother #2: I agree with you man, now my old lady is riding my back about me finding a job. She doesn't understand that no one wants to hire black men!

Brother #3: Man, I'm really tired of this shit. People are always putting us down and not giving us a fair chance. I give up. I think I'll go buy me a forty-ounce and hang out at the park.

You know what I'm talking about don't you? Now I'm sure some of you are saying that I'm perpetuating the myth of the stereotypical black male, but that isn't true. I am well aware that the majority of us are hard-working, and will definitely work if given the opportunity. I have experienced the powerlessness of being rejected because of my color, but I refused to let those experiences dictate my destiny. The point I want to make is, if you catch yourself in that conversation, I want you to interrupt it and change the way you're thinking. You must realize that the more you keep telling yourself how bad things are, the worse they're going to get. Remember the power of belief. If you start believing you can improve the situation you will. Let's go back to our three brothers and see what could happen if they chose to think differently.

Brother #1 Man, it's so hard being black in this country. A brother doesn't stand a chance.
Brother #2 You know I've been doing some thinking lately, and I was wondering how the

brothers felt during the fifties and sixties. Although they had a lot of obstacles they still found a way to open a lot of doors for us.

Brother #3 *You're right man, I can't imagine what it would have been like to have to sneak around to read. Having to walk through the back door all the time and to be constantly thrown out of public places.*

Brother #1 *I guess you're right, rather than sit here and feel sorry for myself I'm sure I can find something to do. Even if it's just reading a book.*

Brother #2 *Man that's a great idea. Have you heard about that new book by Michael Taylor. Everybody's been talking about it. I hear it's got some very positive and empowering suggestions on how to change your life.*

Brother #3 *What are we waiting for? Let's get busy and make something happen in our lives. We can do it if we put our minds to it. Let's commit ourselves to thinking positive and following positive examples and role models. I don't know about you guys but I feel an internal shift that says I can live my dreams if I choose to.*

We live in such a pessimistic, cynical society it's extremely difficult for some people to believe that these types of conversations actually exist. I promise you that they do. But if you hadn't participated in one, I suggest that you take the initiative and start one.

3. THE "THAT'S WHAT WHITE PEOPLE DO" MENTALITY

This belief is probably as destructive as the previous one. What makes this one so powerful is the fact that it's seldom verbalized. It grabs you unconsciously and causes you to give up on your dreams and aspirations. Remember at the beginning of this chapter when my friend told me I couldn't surf? The truth was, he didn't have any evidence that this was true. He simply had a belief that white people would keep me from surfing. Of course there was a time when we were not allowed to participate in certain things, but that was then and this is now. Now ask yourself honestly: Is there something I've been wanting to do but I talked myself out of it because I believed only white people did it?

Here are some examples of some things that I've heard brothers say only white people do.

1. Become billionaires
2. Surf
3. Scuba dive
4. Rock climb
5. Snow ski
6. Participate in gymnastics
7. Sky dive
8. Have monogamous relationships
9. Enjoy nature
10. Travel around the world
11. Exercise

The "That's What White People Do" Mentality

12. Retire at forty
13. Meditate
14. Play golf
15. Enjoy classical music
16. Enjoy the Arts and Theatre
17. Get their Ph.D.
18. Go to spiritual retreats
19. Start their own company
20. Write positive motivational books

Take a moment and ask yourself if there is something on this list that you've really wanted to do but talked yourself out of it because you were afraid of being labeled a sellout. Of course that list could go on forever, so think about some things that you've stayed away from. Ask yourself right now: "Is there something I've really wanted to do but I talked myself out of it because I was afraid of being rejected by my peers? Have I been afraid of being labeled a 'Sellout' by my brothers and therefore let my dreams float away?" Is there a part of you that's been saying "Go for it!"? Don't worry what other people think, just do it? If you feel something move inside, you're on the right track. There is a part of you that knows you've got great potential. The key is trusting yourself, not the people around you. Sometimes it only takes a little nudge and then a person will allow themselves to take a risk and follow their heart. I hope you will trust your own instincts.

I believe the biggest sellout is the man who allows other people to dictate what he can or cannot do. "A sellout" is someone who is more concerned with looking good in front of his peers rather than following his heart and chasing his dream.

That reminds me of a movie I've seen. Have you seen the movie *White Men Can't Jump*? It's the story about a black guy (Wesley Snipes) and a white guy (Woody Harrelson) who put together this basketball con game. The way it worked was: Wesley would go to your neighborhood playground and start talking all this trash about what a great player he was. He would say that he could beat anybody on the court by himself. After he roused up the players, eventually someone would challenge him. But since they were playing two on two ball he needed a second man. Of course the setting was in an all black area and Woody would be the only white guy around. So Wesley would say that he was so great that he was willing to even take the scraggly looking white guy. (Here's another example of beliefs. Most of the guys had the belief that white guys couldn't play, so they would gladly let Wesley take the white guy.) It turned out that the white guy was a great player, and they would win most of their games, and win a lot of money in the process.

During the movie the white guy makes a very powerful statement. He approaches the black guy and says "Black guys would rather look good and lose, than look bad and win." Take a moment and think about that. Does that apply to you? Is your image more important than living your dreams? Do you make sure that you always look good to gain approval from your friends? Have you invested more time, money and effort in your appearance instead of yourself? Only you can answer that question. Will you answer honestly?

Here's something to remember: "Most people who act like they have a lot of money, don't. Most people who don't act like they have a lot of money, do." Just be honest with yourself. If you choose to live your dreams first, everything else will follow. Don't try to fake it.

When I first started my company, I was talking to a friend about becoming a millionaire. First he didn't take me seriously, then he said "Even if you do make it, the white man is going to take it from you." He was not trying to be malicious; he simply had these limiting beliefs that I couldn't do it. And if I did, that mysterious white man was going to snatch it away from me. Since you and I know that this white man doesn't really exist, I guess that means I'll get to keep my millions. What do you think?

4. HE'S TRYING TO BE WHITE!

If I had a nickel for every time I was accused of trying to be white, the money I would have accumulated by now would probably have exceeded the profits of this book. This is probably the hardest part about being a black male in my opinion. This belief causes alienation and anger, and at times it seems like a no-win situation. As a race of people, we have to learn to accept our own diversity. As more and more of us assume positions of power, we have to learn to accept the fact that there is no longer a "Black way of thinking." Because we choose to be open-minded does not mean we're selling out. We have to be able to base our decisions on our own beliefs and values and not conform to the way most people think we are supposed to think. Without question or hesitation I can honestly say I have never even considered wanting to be white. As my grandfather taught me, I simply needed to think in the way of the man with all the money, not try to be like him. And that's exactly what I've done. All my life I've been attacked by my own people because I chose to speak properly and create the life I knew I deserved. This has to cease. We have to understand that we are individuals and we have the right and the freedom to think and do anything we please. We have to be willing to accept our differences and still support each other.

A good example of what I'm talking about was the selection of Clarence Thomas to the Supreme Court. Before this selection, I had never even heard of Clarence Thomas. I personally am not very active in the political process except during major elections. So when he was nominated, all I knew about him was that he was Black. Although I knew absolutely nothing about his political views, I was very proud of him for his accomplishment. All of a sudden I started hearing things like "Clarence Thomas is whiter than the whitest white man." They attacked him in the paper and called him "Uncle Tom." Some people even marched in protest about his lack of support for black people. I still know very little about the man, but I am still very proud of him. The question I want to raise is: Why can't we, as blacks, oppose someone's views without expelling them from our race? We obviously don't have to agree with his opinions, and we should speak out against his legislation if it isn't beneficial. But do we have to ostracize him and say he isn't black? Whether you like him or not, he is still a black man.

The "That's What White People Do" Mentality

We create a lot of separation amongst ourselves by our unwillingness to allow a black man to make decisions on his own. I believe we are paying a terrible price for these reactions. If we try to make our kids conform to a certain way of thinking how can we expect to move ahead. If our kids feel they have to conform, then we put limits on them and that is a shame. We must allow ourselves and our children to be open-minded and willing to take risks without the fear of expulsion from our race. Our future depends on it.

I have been fortunate in that I have always been exposed to people of other races. I learned very early that all people really are the same if you will take some time to get to know them. I have been blessed with a few white friends whom I would trust with my life, and I am truly grateful to have them in my life. It is now 1994 and the year 2000 will be here before you know it. We must understand the importance of our diversity in this great country of ours. Some of you may have a lot of hatred and anger towards people of other races, but it is now time to lay our differences aside and create unity. It takes a real man to be the first to extend his hand in fellowship, I hope you will do just that.

I have a few questions I would like to ask you;

If a black man chooses to become a millionaire, does that mean he's trying to be white?

If a black man chooses to participate in self-help seminars, does that mean he's trying to be white?

If a black man chooses to be affectionate in public with the woman he loves, does that mean he's trying to be white?

If a black man chooses to participate in his children's lives and doesn't believe in corporal punishment, does that mean he's trying to be white?

If a black man chooses to go bungy jumping, does that mean he's trying to be white?

If a black man chooses to be a republican, does that mean he's trying to be white?

If a black man chooses to be monogamous, and love cherish and adore his mate, does that mean he's trying to be white?

If a black man chooses to attend a majority white church because it really nurtures his soul, does that mean he's trying to be white?

The answer is an emphatic "No!" It simply means that he wants the best for himself and his family, and he deserves the best life has to offer.

We have to stop attacking each other because we choose to do something that is considered out of the norm. We have to accept the fact that the majority of white people in this country aren't racist and would gladly support us if we allowed them to. The time has come for us to not even have this color conversation. It's time to take control of our own destinies and create the life we deserve. We've "struggled" long enough. It's time to make a change and a new commitment to unity.

When you think of the Civil Rights Movement, what one word comes to mind? Freedom? Equality? Power? For me the one word is "ACCESS." When I think of why our brothers gave their lives I realize that they simply wanted "ACCESS." They knew that if they had "ACCESS" to the knowledge and information, then ultimately they could achieve everything their white counterparts had achieved. So now that it's 1994, and we have that "ACCESS," who's responsible for our success? We are! It is completely up to us to take advantage of the doors that are wide open to us today.

Our brothers died so that we could attend the workshops of our choice.

They died so we could create close intimate relationships with our mates.

They died so we could be better fathers and not subject our children to the pain they experienced.

They died so we could base our political views on our own individual beliefs.

They died so we could create strong family units that go on for generations.

They died so we could bungy jump if that is our preference.

And they died so that we could choose a God based on our soul's calling.

So if we aren't taking full advantage of all the opportunities available to us right now, doesn't that mean that our brothers died in vain? To me that is absolutely unacceptable. I choose to take full advantage of every door that is open to me. That is the way that I repay my brothers of whom I am so very proud.

Ultimately as a *Black American* you only have two choices in which you can view our situation. First, you have the choice to view us as victims, a small group of people that is constantly abused, disrespected and on the edge of extinction. Or you can see us as we truly are, a group of people that are the epitome of strength and perseverance. A group of people that knows and lives the word "commitment." A group of people brought to a strange land with nothing but the clothes on their backs; brought to a place that was totally foreign and new. Because of their determination and courage, they were able to adapt, and despite seemingly insurmountable obstacles, they have prospered and cut their niche in a place that tried everything in their power to keep them separate. How my brothers, can you not be empowered by that. What other evidence do you need of our greatness? That in itself should be enough to inspire you to go out into the world with your head held high. So take a moment and acknowledge the greatness within you. You must understand that you are a very important part of history and no one is going to deny us what we deserve. Stand proud, my brothers, and bask in your greatness.

So my recommendation is that we, as Black people, start supporting and empowering each other. We have to remove all these limiting beliefs and start working together. That means with people of all races. Yes, there are still a lot of ignorant people in the world and there are definitely problems that need to be addressed, but the truth is this is the greatest country in the world. We have to stop taking it for granted, and make a commitment to keep it the greatest country there is. I truly love and support this country and will do everything in my power to make sure that my children have the opportunity to know how fortunate they are to live in the good ole U.S.A.

So let's summarize those four limiting beliefs so that you can eliminate them from your consciousness.

1. Black Men are an Endangered Species.
2. The white man is holding us back.
3. The "That's What White People Do" Mentality
4. He's trying to be white.

Make sure that you no longer hold on to these limiting beliefs. I have an analogy I want you to think about. After you read it take a moment and give it some serious consideration. It holds a very important lesson about living your dreams.

Have you ever heard the story of how they train elephants?

When an elephant is first born, they take these huge chains and chain them to the ground. No matter how hard that baby elephant pulls on that chain he can't break free. He pulls and pulls until finally he realizes the futility in his efforts so he gives up. As the elephant gets older they use a smaller and smaller chain on him, but the elephant knows from previous experience that he can't break free. By the time the elephant is full grown, it only takes a small nylon rope to keep him imprisoned, a rope so small that it would only take a minimum amount of effort to break free. Yet he won't do it. He simply stays trapped by an obstacle so small it baffles the mind that an animal that weighs several tons is being held back by a simple rope. So why doesn't the elephant break free? The answer is simple: he just doesn't "Believe" that he can.

So what's holding you back? Is it possible you're just like the elephant? THINK ABOUT IT!

The only true security in life comes from knowing that every single day you are improving yourself in some way.

Anthony Robbins

PERSONAL GROWTH:
AN INVESTMENT IN SELF

My definition of personal growth is: to gain a deeper understanding of one's emotional, spiritual, physical and intellectual self. I believe that if we commit ourselves to gaining this deeper understanding of ourselves, then life can really be filled with joy, love, passion and inner-peace. Unfortunately most males simply refuse to take an honest look at all four areas of their lives. We usually invest in the physical and intellectual, yet neglect the emotional and spiritual. The bad news is, when we do this we miss out on a very important part of ourselves, and until we make a conscious effort to deal with these aspects of our lives, then something will always be missing.

Imagine your life as a wheel that's divided into four equal parts. Each part represents an important part of your psyche that's necessary for your well being. Those four parts are Spiritual, Emotional, Intellectual and Physical. If we choose to develop a deeper understanding of ourselves, then we take time to make sure that all four areas receive our attention and we commit to nurturing each part. If we do this, then the wheel becomes balanced and it rolls along smoothly and our lives work. But when we neglect any one part of the wheel, then it becomes unbalanced, and it can't roll smoothly. What we normally do is neglect one or more parts of the wheel and when our lives reach the area that's been neglected, we simply push over the rough spot and get to the balanced parts. This is called denial.

Have you ever noticed how your life will seem to be going along smoothly without any problems, then all of a sudden your life is in total chaos? Maybe your career takes a turn for the worst or you experience a failed relationship. After a few hardships you push past the rough spots and things seem to be going smoothly again. Pretty soon you repeat the same pattern. Or maybe your career is going smoothly yet you can't enjoy your success because of your health. You could possibly have a great body, yet you can only speak in monosyllabic words so your conversations are limited to an eighth grade level. These are all examples of being unbalanced. When we refuse to deal with the areas in our lives that need special attention, we create patterns that will continue until we address the problem directly.

In a culture that constantly bombards us with images of males being nonemotional and detached, we have produced a phenomenon called "Anhedonia" which means non-pleasure. It is this state of mind that causes a lot of pain in our lives. The reason this state exists is because as males, a large majority of us have disconnected from really feeling our emotions. When we deny our true emotions, we become closed off and distanced in all of our relationships. Without our emotions we cannot experience intimacy, passion or true inner-joy on a deep emotional level. Since most of us are what's been called "Left brain thinkers;" we miss out on the real pleasure of experiencing life the way it was meant to be. Our focus now needs to turn towards balancing that emotional part of ourselves that will allow us to experience deep emotional pleasure. To substantiate this state take this simple test. Find a comfortable place to sit where you won't be interrupted. Make sure you have a clock handy, then sit still and close your eyes. Keep your eyes closed for five minutes. After the five minutes ask yourself how you felt. Were you able to keep your eyes closed? Did time go by quickly or slowly? Did you get impatient and convinced yourself that the exercise was silly so that you could justify opening your eyes? Did you even do the exercise? What were you thinking?

The first time I did this exercise I kept my eyes closed for approximately two minutes, then I decided how silly it was and skipped over it. What I've learned since is, at the time, I truly didn't know how to sit still and relax. I always felt as if I was always supposed to be doing something, and I would feel guilty if I weren't. I was caught in the anhedonic state of not being able to experience pleasure.

As I looked back in retrospect, I found the pattern of not addressing the emotional aspect of myself. At an early age I had decided that the most important thing to me was to own my own company. I invested most of my efforts into gaining knowledge and information on the technical aspect of business. I would read business publications and attend management seminars and always maintained a fitness program that kept me in shape. I nurtured the intellectual and physical sections of my life's wheel but neglected the emotional and spiritual. It wasn't until a tragedy happened in my life that I took the time to address these most important areas of my life. I would like to share with you the circumstances that brought about this realization.

At the age of nineteen I assumed a position with a major building supply retailer. Because of my love for business and the knowledge I had gained over the years, I moved up the corporate ladder rather quickly. By the age of twenty three, I had become one of the youngest managers in the history of the company. During my ascent up the ladder I had made the decision that in order to make it to the top, a person needed to be married in order to show their maturity. Since I felt I had two marks against me, one being black, the other being so young; I decided that being married would give me an advantage. This is definitely one of those societally perpetuated myths; but because of my denial of dealing with my emotions, I bought into it. Anyway I married my current girlfriend at the time and thought I was living the American Dream. I was earning $50,000 per year, bought my first home, had a management position and I was only twenty-three years old.

At the age of twenty six I started to experience burnout. Because of the corporate structure of the company, there was no upper level management. I had peaked, and there was nowhere else to go. I decided to start my own company. I tried a few small ventures that I could pursue from my home. Most of them were related to the construction field. I did attempt a janitorial company, but there was a part of me that couldn't deal with being a garbage man. During this time I began to create friction in my marriage. My wife could not understand why a person making my salary would even consider giving up the security of a major corporation, to take on the risk of starting their own business. We would argue about my dream of being my own boss, but to her it was simply that, a dream.

Personal Growth: An Investment In Self

But to me it was very real. A part of me knew my ultimate destiny and I refused to give up on my childhood dream. I had to trust that inner voice that kept whispering in my mind to follow your heart and chase your dream.

Then everything started to go wrong. The Houston economy took a nose dive because of the oil glut. Because of this I experienced a thirty percent cut in my salary. At the time I had already been trying to live well beyond our means, and it started catching up with me pretty quickly. I was overwhelmed with bills and continued to go deeper and deeper into dept. I maxed out all my credit cards trying to keep my head above water. But I could only rob Peter to pay Paul for so long.

Despite my financial situation, I continued to attempt to start my own company. I hoped that I could create extra revenue for my family, but it didn't work out that way. It actually made things worse. My wife and I were constantly arguing, and it got to the point where we couldn't even communicate. We decided to try counseling, but it was too late. Neither of us were willing to compromise, and the marriage ended in divorce. At this particular time I had no idea what sort of emotional state I was in. I actually denied the whole emotional effects of the entire situation.

I couldn't understand what had happened. Just two years prior I had it all; now I had nothing. All the wonderful pictures that I had painted of my ideal family and business life were now not only tarnished, but nonexistent. I was in foreign territory; for the first time in my life, I had failed. Failure was definitely a new and painful experience. I didn't know what to do. I remember sitting in a restaurant one day and becoming extremely angry at society. I was angry because I had followed society's rules about being successful, yet when I got to the top, I didn't receive the fulfillment that I thought I was entitled to.

Fortunately I have always been solution oriented, so immediately I started to put together a game plan. I needed to consolidate my bills and get out of this financial mess that I was in. But it was too late, I was in too deep; my mortgage company had already begun foreclosure procedures; and since my former spouse couldn't find a job, I was basically trying to support two households. Things just kept getting worse. By now everything was starting to take a toll on me emotionally and psychologically. I had entered into a deep state of depression which, at the time, I didn't even recognize. I couldn't see my way out of the mess. As the bill collectors kept knocking and foreclosure proceedings got closer, I couldn't see my way out. I thought I could keep everyone at bay by kiting my checks, but that caught up to me in a hurry. Then I convinced myself that I could embezzle the money and pay it back later. This definitely made matters worse. At the time I didn't have any close friends that I was comfortable enough to share what I was going through. Eventually the pressure became too great. I knew something had to shift fast. I had begun to lose weight and had really isolated myself. Although I pretended nothing was wrong to my employees, I was literally dying and was too ashamed and embarrassed to ask for help. I started to have fleeting thoughts of suicide, and would dismiss them as silly little thoughts. But the thoughts became more frequent and I became afraid. Without question, my kids were the reason that I held on; I couldn't imagine leaving them and having them tormented by the fact that their dad killed himself. I just would not put that burden on them.

I needed help, but I didn't know where to turn. I wrote a letter to my supervisors and asked if they could possibly loan me some money to help me get back on my feet. I was informed that was against company policies. I needed a miracle, and I needed it quickly.

During this time I really didn't believe in God. All of my experiences with this entity had been extremely negative, and not once did I blame Him. I took complete responsibility for the situation I was in and decided that since I had gotten myself into this mess, then I had to get myself out. (Of course, I know now who was carrying me.)

As fate would have it, I received my miracle. I was sitting up late one night, and I saw an advertisement about depression. I immediately recognized the symptoms, and I realized the organization that ran that ad could help me. The bad news was I was too afraid and too ashamed to go there. (In case you haven't heard, the term is called "Denial," and it had a very strong grip on me.) I decided to give them a call for some information.

I called Baywood Hospital in Clear Lake City. I really didn't know what to say, so I asked the lady if they had some brochures they could send me. She invited me to come tour the facility, but I declined. (Major denial; the thought of asking for help terrified me. I was afraid they would force me to tell them how much pain I was in.) I received some information by mail, but it didn't talk about depression. It only talked about the hospital. There was no way I was going to go there and ask for help, so I blew it off. A week or so passed and I received some divine intervention. A female customer of mine and I were talking, and somehow we started talking about my divorce. She asked how I was doing, and as usual my response was "I'm fine; everything's great." This is denial in its most potent stage. It was the same response I had used all my life. No matter how much pain I was in, I always said "I'm great" (The truth was, I was in so much pain I really wanted to just grab her and cry for a few days.) Fortunately for me, she could see through my facade. "Well, I'm sure your doing okay, but I think it's important that whenever you go through an emotional crisis like divorce, you should at least have a support system to help you through the pain."

"What the hell is 'an emotional crisis?'" I thought to myself. I wasn't going through any emotional crisis, how could I be going through something I knew absolutely nothing about. (I'm sure you recognize the big D word by now.)

"Have you heard of a place called The Center for Recovering Families?" she asked.

"No, what is that?" I asked.

"It's a support center in Houston. They have counselors and workshops that support people who are going through emotional crisis."

There's that damn 'emotional crisis' again. "I wonder what that really means?" I thought to myself.

"Do they deal with depression?" I asked.

"Absolutely. Depression is usually the result of going through an emotional crisis."

Then the lights turned on in my head, and she really had my attention.

Personal Growth: An Investment In Self

"Where is this place?"

"I'll give you their phone number and you can call for directions." I thanked her for the information, and she thanked me for my assistance. I don't remember ever seeing her again, but I can honestly say that she had just saved my life.

I rushed home that evening with anticipation. A part of me knew that this was the answer I was looking for. I called and got directions and I even made an appointment to speak to one of the counselors.

When I got there, I was pleasantly surprised to find an incredible library of books on all types of things dealing with human behavior: depression, child abuse, alcoholism, co-dependence and even spirituality.

I walked around for a while and waited for my appointment. Finally a lady called my name and we went into her office. "What can I do for you?"

"I'm looking for some information on depression and I was wondering if you could make some suggestions."

"Have you been depressed lately?" she asked.

"I'm really not sure," I responded.

"Have you had any emotional trauma in your life recently?"

"Emotional trauma, hmm..., that must be emotional crisis, brother," I thought to myself. "I'm not really sure what you mean by emotional trauma," I answered.

"Have you experienced any of the following: Loss of a loved one. Change in job. Dramatic change in income. Illness. Divorce. Inability to concentrate. Loss of sex drive. Change in sleeping patterns?"

"Not really," I responded. "Oh yea, I forgot, I did go through a divorce a few months ago, but I'm okay." (Do I need to remind you who's speaking for me? Mr. D that's who.)

"Those are a few examples of trauma and their effects," she said.

"Well, I just need to get a little information, so could you just recommend a book and I'll be on my way."

"Are you sure you wouldn't like to speak to one of our counselors about your divorce?"

"I don't think so, but if I change my mind, how much do you charge for your services?"

"We operate on a sliding scale based on your ability to pay."

"Thank you, that's all the information I need. I think I'll go browse through your book store." (This is what denial does to you. As I look back in retrospect, I realize how hard I was trying to get help, I was dying yet I refused to say to anyone "I NEED HELP." If you are in this situation, you must understand that it's okay to ask for help. We live in a society that constantly bombards us with images of men being tough and strong and able to carry the world on our shoulders, but we are paying an incredible price for this in the increased number of alcoholics, suicides, child abuse, single parent homes and homicides. We must do everything we can to curb these problems. Asking for help is the first step. You are not alone. Take a chance. Ask for help. It will make your life a lot easier; I promise.)

I left the counselors office before she had a chance to really ask how much pain I was in.

I walked to the bookstore where I knew I would feel safe. (Remember how much I love reading? Actually that was part of my denial. Reading was a way for me to not feel. It was easy for me to analyze and rationalize, as long as I didn't have to experience the pain.) As I walked around the bookstore, I was intrigued by all the different books. These were a lot different from the business books I had read, but I rationalized it by saying "I'm sure I can figure this out. I just need to find the right book." I walked around and listened to a couple of women having a conversation about 'Inner-Child work.' "I wonder what the hell that is," I thought to myself. This is definitely unfamiliar territory. There were so many books. I didn't know which one to pick or where to start.

Then I received that divine intervention again. I was about to leave when all of a sudden this book started calling my name. (No I didn't really hear my name, but I'm sure you know what I'm talking about.) "Over here!" it called out. "I'm the one you're looking for, I'm the one that can stop all the pain. Pick Me, Pick Me!!!!!!"

It was a book by Charles Whitfield titled *Healing The Child Within*. I had no idea what it was about, but I remembered the conservation I overheard between the two women. I didn't understand why, but I knew it was the one I needed. I bought it. Went home, and started reading.

I know now that there are no accidents. Everything does happen for a reason, and this was a perfect example. I started reading, and couldn't put the book down. It talked about how our childhood set the stage for all our relationships. In the case of abuse, it is necessary to reconnect with that part of you that had been hurt before you can really create close intimate relationships. I stayed up until four in the morning reading. Things were finally starting to make sense. (Have you picked up on my control issues of having to understand everything?)

After reading Whitfield's book, I went back to the center for more information. I literally became obsessed with the whole recovery phenomenon. I started reading everything I could get my hands on.

After several trips and a dozen or so books, I ran across the one that would shift my life for good. It was John Bradshaw's, *Healing the Shame That Binds You*. Although most of the books contained very similar principles, he put a lot of emphasis on participating in groups. He said that in order to truly heal, you have to be able to share your story with other human beings. As I read that I realized that I had always had an aversion to groups. I had never participated in group activities and I had rationalized it by focusing on my company dreams. But the truth was, there was a part of me that felt flawed or defective, and I avoided groups out of fear of being exposed.

So I knew that I had to confront this fear if I wanted to stop the pain. I decided to call a therapist and found one that I felt comfortable with. I made an appointment and, though I was terrified, I kept it.

I walked in and the woman was extremely nice. Of course the first thing I thought of was her wanting my money (which I didn't have anyway), and my heart was beating at a million beats per minute. I asked if they had any black female therapists, and she said no, but if that was really important to me she would locate one. I decided I was okay and we went into her office. I was sweatin' bullets, but I had my best denial defense in place and that false grin that I hid behind was still intact.

The first thing I did was try to prove to her that I was okay. "I would just like a little information," I said.

"What would you like to know?"

"Well I've been doing some research and I've found my role in my family of origin chart. I understand how my abusive childhood has affected my relationships, and I realize that I'm co-dependent. So all you need to do is tell me how to fix things. (In case you haven't figured it out, I was really in denial. I was sitting there trying to prove to this therapist how smart I was by using all this psycho-babble which was my way of avoiding the pain. Once the big D grabs you, it's tough getting it to let go.)

She smiled, told me how smart I was and that she was really impressed with my understanding of the principles. But it didn't have anything to do with my recovery.

"Recovery? What recovery? Who's in recovery? I'm not in recovery. What do you mean 'my recovery?' I'm okay! I'm fine! There's nothing wrong with me. What am I supposed to be recovering from anyway?" (Big D rears its ugly head again.)

"It's all right Michael, calm down. Everything is fine," she responded.

She obviously picked up on my fear and nervousness, and she probably sensed that I was about to run out the door, so she shifted. "I'm really glad you're here and if there's anything you want to talk about then go right ahead. I'm here to listen. Tell me why you're here."

"I told you I just needed to get some information. For example, how much will this cost and how long will it take?"

"How long will what take?" she asked.

"This recovery thing you talked about."

"Well, that depends on you" she said.

"Well, how about a ball park figure — one month, three months, six months? It shouldn't take more than six months; am I right?"

"Michael, you have to believe me, there is really no way of me knowing that. I promise, it's all up to you."

"Okay, I believe you (not really), so how much does it cost?"

"We operate on a sliding scale according to your ability to pay."

"Oh boy, they must be in cahoots with that other organization," I thought to myself.

She showed me a range of prices, and I committed to paying $20 per week, which I really didn't have, but I knew I had to find a way. So after about an hour or so with me running from the real issues, I left and scheduled an appointment for the following week. On my way home something was different, I felt a sense of relief. It was like removing a weight off or something. I had really begun my Recovery.

After three sessions I noticed some changes. I had begun to sleep through the night and I was literally breathing easier. Although my life was still in total chaos, there was hope now, and I had something to look forward to. I had begun to start trusting her, and I started to be more open. She convinced me to start keeping a journal. She said it would help me connect with my thoughts and feelings, and the entries became easier. My journal actually became my closest friend.

During this time I conceived an idea for a new company based on the things I started learning about myself and my recovery. I created an animated character that could be used to help children deal with being in the same situation I experienced, and something inside of me told me this was the dream of my childhood. I hired an artist to do a sketch of the character I conceptualized, and when he put it on paper, I knew I had found my dream.

As irrational as it may sound, I called my supervisor and told them I had to quit. I had no money, creditors breathing down my neck, and still a lot of emotional issues to deal with, but that little voice inside was going on like a Nike™ ad: "Just Do It, Just Do It!!!"

I had no idea how I was going to make it work, but that part of me knew there was no way it wouldn't work. So I started chasing my dream.

Of course, everyone around me told me how crazy I was for leaving my nice secure job, but I've never been one to listen to other people. Besides, I had lost everything already, so what else did I have to lose, except maybe my sanity. (That is definitely a story in itself. Hmm, do you smell something? Hmm, smells like another book to me. Check your bookstores the summer of '95; I'll give you all the details.)

Back to the story:

I was making progress with my therapist; she gave me tapes to listen to and recommended books to read. I was definitely in the healing process.

Then came an unexpected experience.

We had obviously developed a level of trust that she felt would allow me to really deal with some deep pain. I was sitting in her office, and she told me to discuss some of the experiences of my childhood. I started telling her about being separated from my mom and the abuse that was inflicted on me by my grandmother. There was also sexual abuse and verbal abuse by a family friend. As I shared my story with her, I could see the pain and horror in her eyes. Yet I had my usual grin and denial mechanisms in place.

She asked me how I could be smiling while discussing such horrific experiences, and, as usual, I smiled and said, "I'm okay." Then she looked at me and asked, "How would you feel if those things happened to your son?"

I cannot put in words what took place next. It was as if someone had flipped a switch in my mind. All of a sudden I started to cry uncontrollably. It was so instantaneous it still baffles my mind to this day how it happened. All of a sudden I was feeling years and years of repressed pain. As I began to feel that pain, I became afraid that I wouldn't be able to stop it. I went back in my head and tried to figure out what had just taken place.

"How in the hell did you do that?" I asked.

"I didn't do anything," she replied.

"Well explain to me what just happened. Something happened and I want you to tell me what." By now I was really angry. I felt that she was withholding information that could expedite this recovery process. I wanted to know what she had done.

"Michael, even if you understood what happened, it wouldn't do any good. The only way out for you is through the pain. There are no shortcuts. If there was an easier way, I promise, I would tell you. But there isn't. You've been through twenty-eight years of pain and you can't expect to heal that in a day. You have to trust me. I can lead you, but you're the one that has to do the work."

I was upset to say the least. I didn't know what to do. A part of me was saying trust the process, and a part of me was saying there has got to be an easier way.

Being the rational minded in-denial idiot at the time, I decided to prove to her that I could and would figure this out. I told her I didn't need her anymore and that I wasn't coming back. The truth was I was terrified of experiencing that pain. I wanted to avoid it at all cost.

I did what I had been doing all my life. I ran from the pain, but created more in the process. The good news is I at least ran in the right direction. I went back to the center and not only bought more books, but also attended some workshops put on by John Bradshaw.

I continued my reading and research and started participating in "Inner-Child" type workshops. As time progressed my life took a major turn for the better. I started to really feel for the first time in years. It was as if I was encased in this suit of armor that had protected me from the pain, yet restricted my ability to touch people or allow them to touch me. But now I began to shed that armor, and piece by piece I removed my steel cage. Inside I found this incredible wonderchild that had been trying for years to get out. At last he was free! And for the first time, he felt lovable.

Removing that armor was not an easy process. It's taken me three years to get to this point in my life where I can truly say I'm emotionally and psychologically free. During this process I had to be willing to share my pain with others There were times when I had to be completely vulnerable and expose myself by crying and expressing the hurt, and allowing other people to support me and share my pain. It is the sharing and the acceptance of support that allowed me to heal.

The therapist had been right. There are no shortcuts. The only way out was through the pain, but the joy and love I feel now was worth every bit of that pain.

So, after three *years* of recovery and the recognition of the wonderful gift that I am as a person, I finally balanced the emotional part of my life's wheel. There were several major discoveries I made during this process.

First, I realized the reason I had been successful up to this point was because of a fear of being labeled inadequate. Being a workaholic was the way that I could feel good about myself. As long as I was successful, then I had that image to hide behind. The truth was, I created a belief that said people will only love you if you're successful. The thought that someone could love me for me was nonexistent; it was as if I needed accomplishments to be accepted.

Another lesson was the lesson of support. At a very young age I decided that people really couldn't be trusted. I learned to depend on no one but me and found it virtually impossible to ever ask anyone for support. This has to be addressed in greater detail. It is my belief that the three hardest words for any male, and especially black males, to say is "I NEED HELP." This has to change. As I mentioned earlier, we have to understand that we cannot carry the world on our shoulders. We have to realize that it is not a sign of weakness to need help. There are people who are there for us if we will allow ourselves to simply seek the support we need. That support needs to start with our families and friends, and, if necessary, outside help, including therapist and support groups. Whatever it takes, we can no longer walk around emotionally dead. It is that inability to ask for help that pushes us into most of our addictive behaviors, including the misuse of sex, drugs and workaholism. If you are currently involved in some destructive behavior, whatever you do, please understand that it's not your fault, but it is your problem. Take action and get help! Your life can and will get better if you'll allow someone to help.

The very first step to recovery is to surrender. Some of you probably will have difficulty with this (I sure did), but it is essential. I would like to share with you an excerpt from *"Steps for developing a prayer consciousness."* My request is that you think about it for a moment and let it sink in, don't think I'm trying to preach to you, just trust that there may be a message for you.

I Surrender: God is the only power in my life. *I have been attempting to manage my world by trying to control myself, others and the future in separation from my Source. I now see that this does not work. Of mine own self, I can do nothing.* ***I NEED HELP!***

Whatever your belief about God is, use that entity. If you don't believe in God (I didn't at the beginning), trust that there is a power greater than yourself that can and will help, if you will only allow it to.

Without question, that was the hardest part for me. It took me over two years to surrender, but, as soon as I did, the miracles started pouring in from everywhere. I hope you won't be as stubborn as I was.

The greatest lesson I received during my recovery was the understanding and experiencing of true intimacy. Like a majority of men, I always related intimacy with sex. As far as I was concerned I was about as intimate as they came, but the truth was I hadn't a clue. The reason I hadn't experienced intimacy was my lack of trust. You cannot have intimacy without trust. Some of you may need a definition of trust (I certainly did), so I'll do the best I can. First I'll tell you what trust isn't (in an emotional context).

I used to believe that trust was sharing material things, and realizing that your friends would always return them. For example, if I let my girlfriend borrow my brand new jeep without worrying about it, that meant I trusted her. Or if my best male friend needed to stay at my place for a week or so, I could leave valuable things lying around without worrying about him taking them. That meant I trusted him. Both situations obviously take a level of trust, but it's not emotional.

Personal Growth: An Investment In Self

For me now, trust is my ability to go to my friends and say I'm in emotional pain. Maybe I miss my kids and I'm feeling lonely, or my relationship with a significant other isn't going well. Maybe my friend really pissed me off and I can get angry at him without the fear of him not being my friend anymore. The ability to just express my feelings, and to be who I am, and not having to monitor what I say for fear of being rejected. Realizing that I'm not perfect, and that I don't have to have all the answers. The ability to "IN-TO-ME-SEE" all my flaws and inadequacies, and to be able to share the bad as well as the good. When I can look into the eyes of my mate and say "I need you to be here for me emotionally," then I have created intimacy. I didn't have a clue to what these things meant four years ago.

So for the first time in my life, I can honestly say I feel complete. At the present I don't have all the material possessions, but I experience incredible levels of joy and serenity and there's no comparison between the two. I'll take The Joy over The Stuff any day.

Without question, the emotional part of our life's wheel is the most neglected, as far as men are concerned. As I've mentioned, we live in a society that constantly tells us men are tough and emotionless, but it is this belief that leads to so much pain in our lives. When was the last time you've seen a man be vulnerable and expose himself on television. (For those of you who answered several times and thought I was speaking about exposing a physical part of the male anatomy, this section is definitely for you.) If you look at the majority of male characters on television, you'll find that most of them are pretty emotionless when it comes to intimacy. Especially the black male characters! For the most part we're depicted as basketball playing, crotch grabbing, rap singing, woman abusing males. (Remember, this book is about success, so I won't dwell on all the things that are obviously wrong with this society.) So the questions I pose are:

How about your emotional part of life? Is it something that you're even aware of?

When was the last time you took an inventory of your emotional self?

Are you really happy?

Have you ever experienced true emotional joy?

When was the last time you had an emotional experience with your significant other that you allowed yourself to really be supported?

When was the last time you cried?

Have you ever allowed yourself to laugh until you cried?

Have you ever gone to a friend and shared something that you did that you're really ashamed of?

Have you ever allowed yourself to cry in front of a friend because of emotional pain?

Have you allowed your friends or significant other to lean on you?

Are you able to just be a good listener?

Do you turn to your significant other in times of crisis?

How do you feel about discussing your problems with a therapist or in a support group?

Would you be willing to try therapy or counseling?

Are you anesthetizing your pain with drugs or alcohol?

Are you currently having an affair?
Do you have close friends that you can really share openly with?
Have you ever contemplated suicide?
Does your situation in life seem hopeless?
Are you currently depressed and find it difficult to concentrate on your work or family?
Are the bill collectors constantly harassing you for late payments?

These questions can let you know if you are currently involved in an "emotional crisis." Don't let the term scare you the way it did me. It simply means that the emotional part of your life's wheel is unbalanced. The question now becomes: "What are you going to do about it?"

My suggestion is that you take action and get help. Once you make the decision to change, the healing process begins and you're on your way to happiness. I want you to know that you are not alone. There are people out there who care about you. It's a simple matter of asking for their support. The ball is in your court.

Now that we've covered the symptoms, let's talk about solutions. As I've mentioned, dealing with our emotional selves can be difficult. The good news is, there are always solutions. I personally am a big advocate of inner-child work, and I suggest you give it a try. I've spent most of my life keeping myself motivated and practicing positive thinking, but the true happiness didn't come until I decided to deal with the origins of my behavior. Once I saw how I had established the patterns of my self-destructive behaviors, I was able to break those destructive patterns and replace them with healthy ones.

A good example of this is by doing what's called a "Family of origin chart." What the chart does is allow you to recognize how you fit into your family unit, and the certain roles that each child plays within that unit.

My role on the chart was the over responsible super achiever. All my life I focused on achieving things to try and fill that emptiness inside. I created a belief that said people will only love you if you are a high achiever, so I busted my tail off trying to get everyone's approval by being successful. This caused incredible pain in my life. No matter if people told me they cared about me just for me, I had created this belief that I had to have all these accomplishments first, before I could be loved. A perfect example of this is an argument I had with my former wife. We had just purchased our new home and I was extremely proud of my accomplishment. My former wife looked at me and said "Michael, I would still love you even if we were still living in our little apartment. This house is nice but it's just material things. You're what's really important!" I know now she meant that with all her heart, but, at the time, I was in a totally different emotional space. This is what I interpreted: "This woman doesn't appreciate this wonderful house I'm giving her. I can't believe it. Here I am working my ass off to give her all these nice things and she doesn't even appreciate them."

I became extremely angry and didn't talk to her for quite some time. I was totally wrong. It was my own sense of inadequacy that didn't allow me to accept the fact that she really could and did love me just for me, not my material possessions.

This is one of the many lessons I learned by doing inner-child work. Like I said, it's great

Personal Growth: An Investment In Self

to attend these motivational, get-you-pumped-up type seminars, but until you decide to deal with the real issues, you're really just fueling your inadequacies. At least that's what I did.

I believe that John Bradshaw is the leading authority on this subject. If you can't do his workshops, there are several professionals that use his philosophy for the basis of their work. Check around and get some information. I highly recommend that you purchase his book *Homecoming*, and get a good friend or spouse to go through the exercises with you. This book had a more profound affect on me than any other book I've ever read. But you have to be committed to go through the pain.

Don't limit yourself to John Bradshaw alone. He just happens to be my favorite. Just locate inner-child workshops in your area and start asking questions. Another good book is *Healing the Child Within* by Charles Whitfield. *Co-Dependent No More* by Melodie Beattie is also a good book to start with. Claudia Black is another person that was instrumental in providing me with guidance towards my recovery. Her book *Double Duty* is easy to understand, and gives incredible insight into the effects of being raised in an alcoholic environment. In my opinion, she is the leading authority in the "Adult Children of Alcoholics" movement.

Remember what happened to me? I tried to figure it all out in my head by reading all these different books, I don't want you to make the same mistake. The real healing comes from sharing your story with others, realizing you're not alone and allowing yourself to be supported. John Bradshaw calls this "Creating that interpersonal bridge between two human beings." It works.

There are also thousands of twelve step programs all across the country, in churches, schools. You name it, they are available. You simply have to make a commitment to yourself that you're tired of being in pain. Choose to enjoy life the way it is meant to be.

The choice is yours alone. What do you choose?

A word of caution. After you become involved with inner-child work, you may be inclined to blame your parents for treating you poorly. That is not the purpose of your participation. Our parents did the very best they could with the tools they were given, so don't take the victim mentality and create blame. Use the opportunity to take responsibility for your happiness and break the cycle of the mistreatment. Remember, you are completely responsible for your own happiness. No one else is to blame. I have to reemphasize the importance of *self responsibility*. We live in a society that constantly blames everyone and everything else for our problems, especially in the black community. As I mentioned, there is no one or no thing that's going to keep you from participating in the workshops except you. You will probably notice that there aren't many (if any) black participants. You have to know that those people there are hurting just as much as you are. They really are not concerned with your color. As a matter of fact, I can promise you they will be extremely supportive and welcome you with open arms if you allow them to. Trust your instincts. Follow your heart and know that Life is meant to be good, but no one said it would be easy.

Here's an analogy for you to consider:

There was a tribe in the Amazon that was trying to figure out a way to trap monkeys. One obviously intelligent tribesman decided that he would dig holes in the ground with openings just large enough for a monkey's hand to fit in. In the bottom of the holes he placed the monkeys' favorite snack, NUTS. At night the monkeys would come out, smell the nuts and stick a hand in a hole to retrieve the nuts. But remember, each opening was just large enough for their tiny little hand to go in; when they grabbed the nuts they had to clinch their fists, which made their hands too large to get back out through the opening. To escape they each would have to let go of their prize. But being stubborn creatures, they wouldn't let go. In the morning the tribesman would grab the monkeys and have them for dinner.

So in order to be emotionally free you have to be willing to let go of your nuts (Issues). It's a very paradoxical situation. It's so simple, yet it's probably the hardest thing you'll ever do.

THINK ABOUT IT!!!!

After you decide to let go of your nuts, then it's time to really get committed to personal growth.

As human beings we have an infinite capacity for learning. There is no such thing as learning too much. Unfortunately most people think they are supposed to stop learning once they reach a certain age or after they finish college. Nothing could be further from the truth. Success in the 90's is "Constant And Never-ending Improvement" or *CANI™(pronounced kuhn-eye), as the great motivational expert Anthony Robbins puts it. We must become committed to improvement if we hope to create extraordinary success in our lives. So ask yourself, when was the last time I did something to improve myself? Now, if you thought about that $200 dollar shirt or that $900 Armani Suit you just bought, you are on the wrong path. Our society tells us that having these external things shows that we're successful, but the reality is, they don't. I'm not saying not to have these things by any stretch of the imagination, what I'm saying is if you feel that clothes and material things are an investment in personal growth, you're wrong. These are all external symbols, they do nothing for the internal spiritual or intellectual aspect of ourselves.

Here are a few examples of what I mean by personal growth:

1. Do you own a reader's discount card from your local bookstore? If your answer is no, you're a couple of paces behind the group that's headed for success in the nineties. The simplest step in personal growth is reading. When was the last time you bought a new book? What type of personal library do you own? Do you only read sport magazines? How much time do you spend reading on a weekly basis? Reading is exercise for your brain, so are you giving your brain a good workout on a consistent basis?

2. When was the last time you took a new class of some sort? Maybe a foreign language or a computer course, or how about a scuba diving class? Your brain is always ready to expand. Are you giving it that opportunity?

3. Does your Company offer classes that may help you get a promotion? Have you done anything that may get you a few steps higher on that corporate ladder?

These are the areas that affect personal growth. You can choose to do the same thing over

*CANI™ is a trademark of Robbins Research.

and over and wait for that societal safety valve called retirement, or you can create a life filled with passion and fulfillment. The choice is yours.

I would like to make some suggestions: READ and READ and READ some more. There is absolutely no excuse for you not to read. If you don't have any money, go to the library. If you haven't challenged your intellect in awhile, take a new course. There are hundreds of courses you can take through your local college system. Get off your behind and get busy. Of course if being a couch potato is your passion, so be it. But remember "If you keep doing what you've always done, you'll keep getting what you've always gotten."

If you decide you want to get out of your rut and take some action, here are a few suggested readings:

37 Things Every Black Male Should Know	by Errol Smith,
Think and Grow Rich, A Black Choice	by Dennis Kimbro,
Live Your Dreams!	by Les Brown,
Awaken The Giant Within	by Anthony Robbins,
Wealth 101	by John Rogers and Peter McWilliams,
The Power of Positive Thinking	by Norman Vincent Peale.

If you really want to make a shift in your life, I recommend personal growth seminars. Dale Carnagie offers some wonderful courses dealing with personal effectiveness. My favorite and the course that had the second most profound affect on my life after my inner-child workshops is Lifespring. It is a series of personal development workshops that will propel you to live your dreams. During this workshop, not only did I find my purpose, but it taught me what commitment really means. I learned that outside circumstances have absolutely nothing to do with my success. The only thing that matters is what I'm committed to. It was this course that taught me how to follow my heart and live my dreams. I highly recommend that you take this course; it can shift your life dramatically. Anthony Robbins also has several workshops, and though I haven't participated in any, I do have an autographed copy of his book which is one of my most cherished possessions. I'm sure it would be a good investment. I do plan on doing his firewalk one day if he still offers it.

Toastmasters is also a great tool for personal growth. It teaches public speaking and is a very well organized group of people who are committed to eliminating the fear of speaking in public. It is an excellent opportunity for growth. (Hello, UNITY TOASTMASTERS, I LOVE YOU ALL).

These are just a few of the literally hundreds of opportunities that are available for you to expand your horizons. The choice is yours. Will you sit back and let everyone else reap the benefits of living in such a wonderful country? Or will you be amongst the ones who are living their dreams and creating a life that is truly worth living?

Remember; Success in The 90's is your choice.

When you meet anyone, remember it is a holy encounter. As you see him, you will see yourself. As you treat him, you will treat yourself. As you think of him, you will think of yourself. Never forget this, for in him you will find yourself or lose yourself.

A Course In Miracles

RELATIONSHIPS

As I watched the past presidential election, I heard an incredible amount of people discussing family values. Although it was the focal point of most conversation, I don't recall hearing anyone give a clear concise definition of what family values are. I came to the conclusion that there really isn't a definitive answer. It is a matter of personal choice and the answer is as varied as the ethnic makeup of our country. But there is one thing that cannot be disputed, and that is a family always begins with a relationship. So in order to create strong healthy family units, we must develop strong healthy relationships.

Of course there are several types of relationships, professional, romantic, spiritual, friendly to name a few, but they all consist of two common denominators: you and another human being. I want to use this chapter to focus on relationships of the romantic type. It is probably the most important, yet most of us never really give it any real consideration or attention.

It is now time for us to make a new commitment to having meaningful monogamous, loving relationships that last a lifetime. I realize that some of you may not believe this is possible, but I assure you that it is. It is my belief that the ultimate human experience is to find your Soul-Mate and fall head over heels in love and spend the rest of your wonderful lives together. Although it took me over four years to come to this conclusion, I am happy to announce that I have definitely found my Soul-Mate and without question it has brought me joy and happiness which cannot be described in words. Before I go into details about how I found her, I would like to share with you the lessons I learned that allowed me to create the woman of my dreams.

After my divorce, the first words out of my mouth were "I am never going to get married again." (Sound familiar?) Of course, my male ego kicked in and rationalized it by saying that I was now free to play the field. The truth was I didn't want to experience the pain of divorce again, so I was really unconsciously setting myself up to avoid that pain. At first I went into isolation, and threw myself into my work. I didn't date for several months because I felt like I had this huge D stamped on my forehead. The most painful part of my divorce was the experience of failure. I had never really failed at anything in my life and this was a major blow. Of course there's the embarrassment and humiliation of having to tell all your friends that you failed and that really hurt. After several months I decided that it was my responsibility as a man to be in a relationship. Since I have never been shy, finding a date was relatively easy, but my first relationship after my divorce was a complete disaster. The woman I was dating was very supportive. She tried to get me to open up to her, but at the time there was still too much pain. She knew that I wasn't ready to be involved in an emotional relationship, and when she tried to relay that to me I became extremely defensive. I told her that I had laid the ground rules early, and she had agreed to adhere to them.

The ground rules were as follows:
Rule 1: I have no problem with monogamy, so I expect the same from you.
Rule 2: I love great conversation, so be ready to discuss any and everything.
Rule 3: I have a great sense of humor and love to laugh, so be prepared to giggle.
Rule 4: I love to support people, so feel free to say whatever you feel.
Rule 5: I do not want any emotional attachment. You can lean on me, but don't expect that to be reciprocated. Breaking this rule overrides all other rules and will result in the termination of this relationship. So rule #5 was broken, and I ran like a scalded dog.

That relationship lasted approximately two months.

The next relationship lasted about six months, but she broke rule #5, and off I went into the wild blue yonder.

I was getting tired of this relationship game, and had almost come to the conclusion that there wasn't such a thing as a good relationship. As far as I was concerned, it was a societally forced phenomenon that was designed to cause massive amounts of pain. So I chose not to participate for awhile. After a few months I gathered some new insight and decided to give relationships one more try. A very good friend of mine had set me up on a blind date. I really trusted her judgement, so I figured I really didn't have much to lose.

My date and I met at a restaurant. I was very impressed by her physical appearance. She was extremely attractive, and after our conversation began, I realized she was intelligent and confident also. After a three hour conversation we decided to see each other again. As I left the restaurant, I was glad I hadn't given up on relationships. A part of me knew that she was a very special lady. We started spending a lot of time together, and for the first time in what seemed like years, I had something to be happy about. She was wonderful. With her I could be myself and we spent a lot of time just being silly. Our situations were very similar and we had a lot of things in common. Then I started to remember how my other relationships had turned out, and I knew I needed to lay down my ground rules. To my surprise she had no objections to any of them, as a matter of fact she had the same exact rules herself. Boy, was I happy. This was the perfect relationship, in my opinion. I didn't have to risk being hurt emotionally, and I had the freedom to do as I pleased. It just didn't get any better than that.

Things were going extremely well, although we agreed that we could see other people, we spent most of our free time together. Of course, when you spend quality time with someone the way we did, there is no way you can avoid developing some emotional attachment. And that is exactly what started to happen. I truly loved being with her. As a matter of fact, I began to fall in love with her. Of course I couldn't tell her that because I had set the ground rules, and I knew they worked both ways. I surely didn't want to risk losing her, so I kept my feelings to myself.

Then one night, while we were together, she embraced me and said, "I love you, Michael." Although I felt the same way, I reacted totally differently.

"Why did you have to say that?" I asked.

"Because I mean it, that's why," she responded.

"But you know the ground rules. We both agreed that there would be no emotional bonds between us."

"I don't care about the damn ground rules, I've been trying to keep how I feel about you inside but I can't do it any longer. If that's a problem for you, then I'm sorry. But I can no longer hide how I feel about you. We've spent the last year pretending to be just friends, but you and I both know that it's a lot deeper than that. Do you think that I'm just having sex with you? Well I'm not, I'm making love to you, and they're not the same. So, be totally honest, how do you feel about me?"

"Well, I didn't mean for it to happen this way, but I love you too. It's been a long time since I've been happy, and you have been the source of that happiness. I've been wanting to say 'I love you,' but I was afraid that it would scare you away. I'm really glad that you shared how you feel about me because now I can do the same."

That's what my heart wanted to say but because of my past failed relationships and my fear of getting emotionally close, this is what came out:

"I really like you a lot, but I'm not ready for any type of commitment. I realize we have fun together, but I've got a lot of things to deal with right now. The last thing I need to deal with is the complexities of a committed relationship. Remember, we both agreed on that at the beginning."

"I don't give a damn about what we agreed on at the beginning. I'm talking about right now. How do you feel right now? I'm not asking for a committed relationship; I'm not asking to take up any more of your time; I'm not going to make your life any more complex than it is right now. I simply want to know how you feel at this very moment. Would you please give me an honest answer?"

"I don't know. I really don't want to talk about this right now. Why did you have to bring this up in the first place. Everything was perfect. Now you've ruined everything."

"I haven't ruined or changed anything. I'm asking you a very simple question. Do you love me?"

"I honestly don't know. I enjoy your company and I look forward to the times that we're together. But I honestly don't know if I love you or not."

There was silence, and I knew I had just lost the woman that I really loved. As I lay beside her, my heart really wanted to tell her, but the words would not come out of my mouth. I felt a deep sadness, and I knew it was the last time we would be together. I tried to hold her, but she was cold as ice. I knew I had no one to blame but myself.

At the time, I had no idea why it was impossible for me to tell her how I felt. But after really addressing my emotional issues, I've come to realize that the reason I couldn't tell her how I felt was because of my fear of intimacy. I was afraid that if I really told her how I felt, she would ultimately do as all the other women had done in my life. Leave!! The sad part about that was she really didn't want to leave, she honestly loved me, and wanted nothing more than to share her love with me. I was the one that pushed her away. There is a saying that goes: "If one person calls you a jackass, don't worry about it, but, if two or more do, then you had better get a saddle." I knew that it was time for me to get a saddle. As I looked at my past failed relationships, there was one common denominator, "Me." And I committed myself to dealing with my own "Stuff " so that I could create the type of relationships I knew I deserved.

Take a moment and ask yourself if you see the same pattern in your relationships. I wanted to share that story because we must understand that all relationships start with us. At the beginning I was blaming the women I was dating for being the problem, but the truth was, I was the one who needed to address my own fears. It takes an incredible amount of honesty to take responsibility for creating great relationships. But as I've mentioned the first relationship we must develop is the one with ourselves. So I would like to make some suggestions in creating great relationships. First, we must get to know ourselves. As simple as that sounds it is the key to creating great relationships. As I mentioned in the previous chapter, it's taken me three years to get to a point where I honestly feel emotionally healthy. During that time I found out things about myself that I had never considered. I'm not saying that it's going to take you three years, but if you are really committed to creating great relationships, you're going to have to invest some time in getting to know yourself. The first thing we need to know is, what sort of emotional state we're in. And that's going to take some inner work.

Do yourself a favor and commit to doing some personal growth workshops. If you are just getting out of a relationship, take some time alone and ask yourself how you participated within your last one. Notice any patterns you may have created. How long are your relationships lasting? Are you attracting the same type person each time? Never jump immediately from one relationship to another without taking responsibility for how you interacted in the last one. If you do, you are setting yourself up for failure. I realize most people are terrified of being alone and they will usually settle for the old B.T.N. relationship. You know that one don't you? The "Better Than Nothing" relationship. This is why so many people are miserable. Never settle for less than you deserve. If you choose to deal with your own stuff first, I can promise you that you will attract a much better relationship in the long run.

Once you decide to address your own issues, it's amazing how all of a sudden the quality of people you attract magically increase. Learning to love yourself unconditionally will guarantee that you will attract someone that will reciprocate that love. As the saying goes: "You can't give away something you don't have!" Think about that awhile.

The reason I was so optimistic about creating my Soul-Mate was because I chose to focus on my own "Stuff" first. Then I knew I was ready to create the love affair of my life. So my suggestion to you is to do the same. A good way to look at this is by rating yourself on an emotional scale. Ask yourself where you are emotionally on a scale of one to ten. If you know you are a number four, then you will only attract number four women into your life. But if you choose to do some inner work and become a ten then you will attract a ten. I can guarantee you that a number four person will never find a number ten, so don't waste your time. You will always attract the same caliber of mate based on where you are emotionally.

Relationships

We live in a society that constantly bombards us with messages and images of how relationships are supposed to be. But have you ever noticed they are never the way they appear on television or in the movies?

Here are some of the messages that our media constantly throws at us about relationships.

Zales tells us that if we really love our mates, then we should buy them diamonds.

F.T.D. says to show our love we, should send them flowers.

Carnival says that if we will only take one of their cruises, then we will have a great time with no hassles and our relationship will be romantic and filled with excitement.

(I wonder if there have ever been surveys done on relationships that have broken up because of vacations.)

The point is these images convince us that material things and things outside of us are what's needed to make a relationship work. But the truth is these are only external symbols we use to try and express how we feel about a person. They really have nothing to do with the true experience of love. I'm not saying that they aren't important, what I'm saying is they're just symbols. Unfortunately most of us buy into this erroneous belief and try to show our love by buying material things.

This was the trap that I was caught in. (I believe most men are.) As I mentioned in the previous chapter, I thought that by buying my former wife material things, she should have known that I loved her. At the time it was the only way I knew how to express love. And the truth was, I simply couldn't receive her love at the time. But I have come to know that she needed me to be there for her on an emotional level, but I simply didn't have the "emotional tools" at the time. These emotional tools are the keys to creating great relationships. We must understand that we can express how we feel and still retain our masculinity. There is no way that you can create intimate, loving, caring open communication without these tools. So that's why I am advocating doing some inner work, because it will allow you to address any hidden beliefs and emotional scars that may be keeping you from developing close relationships.

Here's a simple test to validate what I'm talking about. Walk up to your mate and look her straight in the eye. Make sure you have her undivided attention. Now ask her sincerely: "Is it more important for me to give you material things, or would you rather me look you in the eye and tell you that I really love you with all my heart, and know that that is the truth?" If you can't do that, ask yourself why not, and see if you are really committed to creating great relationships.

After I decided to do my inner work I realized that the majority of my relationships with women were very shallow and superficial. As a matter of fact I didn't really have true relationships with women unless I was in a romantic relationship with them. I had a belief that if I was involved in a relationship with a female, it was always supposed to turn sexual. This is definitely one of those societally transferred myths. It took me awhile before I could remove this belief from my psyche. But I'm happy to say I've definitely got a handle on it now. I have very open relationships with women now at a level I couldn't have dreamed possible four years ago. Creating these types of relationships means that even if a woman is interested in me sexually, it doesn't mean I have to respond the same way. Some of you may not agree with that or maybe you're saying "If a fine woman walked up to him and offered to have sex with him, he'd jump on it in a New York minute. But the truth is I wouldn't. I no longer have to try and prove my manhood by acting out sexually. Four years ago it would have been a different story, but now, it's absolutely no problem at all.

So ask yourself honestly how you feel about that.

Are you able to have relationships with women that you find physically attractive without the pressure of thinking you are supposed to sleep with them?

Do your hormones go into overdrive every time you interact with a female?

Creating great relationships means being completely honest with yourself and the people you interact with. Are you willing to be completely honest?

Dealing with these issues was not an easy task for me. I was constantly confronted by my ego trying to convince me that I really didn't need intimacy or emotional attachment in my relationships. I was caught in the love 'em and leave 'em trap. But eventually the emotional pain became too great, and the emptiness I was experiencing inside took control and said, "You deserve great intimate, emotionally healthy relationships, so take the time and go inside and there you will find the treasure you seek." So, as I've mentioned, all the answers are within you. You simply have to become committed to creating great relationships in your life.

Let's ask some questions about your relationships. Take a moment and simply think about each question. The key is being honest. If you choose not to be honest with yourself, you can never expect to have great relationships.

1. What are your beliefs about relationships? Do you think that there is no such thing as a great relationship? Do you think all women can't be trusted?
2. Is there constant fighting and screaming within your relationship? Is there physical abuse?
3. Is your relationship built on trust, openness and honesty? Are you comfortable ex pressing how you feel about your mate? Do you know how you honestly feel about your mate?
4. Are you currently involved with more than one person sexually?
5. Are you currently involved in a B.T.N. relationship because you're afraid to be alone?

Take some time and simply think about these questions. A lot of times we are stuck on automatic and we don't even realize there may be another way to look at things. If you are committed to having great relationships you have to be willing to look at things from a new perspective. I will assert to you at this time that the new perspective should be that relationships don't have to be laborious, monotonous, painful experiences. They can and should be exciting, passionate and fulfilling. So, how committed are you anyway? Remember: "If you keep doing what you've been doing, you'll keep getting what you've always got."

Relationships

As I've mentioned before, I don't claim to have all the answers, but I would like to make some suggestions on how you can create healthy relationships. (These suggestions must be preceded by getting to know yourself and doing your inner work first.)

Begin with where you are. If you are currently involved in a relationship, ask yourself what type of words you use to describe your mate. The words we use say a lot about the overall feelings of the relationship. If you are using words like: bitch, old lady, whore, wench or slut; What kind of feelings do you associate to those words? Although you may think that it's only words, I can promise you that if you are using such a negative list to describe your mate, the majority of your experiences with that person are going to be negative. On the other hand if you choose to use positive nurturing words like: sweetheart, honey, sugar puddin', lover or soul-mate; what feelings do you associate with those words? Simply using positive supportive words to address your mate can shift your relationship dramatically. Make it a point to *never* use the negative words.

I believe that one of the most powerful things a person can do to improve a relationship is to relinquish the need to be right. As a whole our culture has conditioned most men to only think in black and white and to take firm positions on their beliefs. In some situations this may (or may not) be appropriate, but within the realm of relationships, I say it just doesn't work. Of course there will be things that you believe in very strongly and should choose not to compromise, but I'm talking about the little trivial things that cause unnecessary friction in relationships. I realize most men won't agree with this, but a good example of what I'm talking about would be the toilet seat issue. I realize we sometimes forget and obviously it really perturbs our mates, so why don't we just put the thing down. I don't want to start a debate over this, but my point is, there are little things that we bring up that are really unnecessary. As men we can just let it pass without having a conniption fit. That may be a bad example, but I'm sure you understand my point. Of course there should be give and take on both sides, so all you women who are reading this take heed. All I'm really saying is when we take the time to get to know ourselves and find a mate to share our lives with, we need to do whatever it takes to make the relationship work. Simply being a little flexible and non-righteous can be a major enhancement to any relationship.

Is it really possible for a relationship to stay loving and passionate forever? I believe so. And I will now share with you the secret to make it happen. Are you ready? This is the big one! Always remember: **"If it's not growing, then it's dying!"** This is the key for developing a relationship that will last a lifetime.

This is a universal principle that applies to every living thing in the universe. So I'm assuming that you are alive (although you may not feel like it) and so is your relationship. So you must keep it growing by nurturing it and loving it. Have you ever noticed when you first meet someone there is this incredible amount of energy you feel inside. You are always excited to see that person and it takes a team of wild horses to keep your hands off of her. Your thoughts are filled with love and passion and you can't seem to think about anything else.

Then after a couple of weeks or maybe months you start to lose that energy. All of a sudden complacency sets in and that energy goes away. Now your thoughts seem to sort of drift back and forth to all the complexities of life and pretty soon you aren't even thinking about all the energy you had at the beginning. All of a sudden you meet someone new and you feel that same energy again. Your thoughts are once again dominated by this new person and you feel alive again. You tell the first person that you have found the right person for you and you're really sorry things didn't work out, but you just know this is the one you've been looking for. Pretty soon it's the same story, the energy goes away and you start looking somewhere else so you can feel that energy again. The truth is that energy that you feel can stay there if you choose to grow the relationship. Whenever you start losing that energy that means the relationship has stopped growing and remember "If it's not growing, it's dying". So the secret is to keep it growing. So how do you keep it growing?

First of all, I think you need to be honest with yourself and ask if you really want your relationship to grow. It could be that your relationship has died and you've simply refused to bury it. So first and foremost make that decision. Be honest with yourself.

After you've made that decision, why not try a relationship seminar? I realize that makes most men tremble, but the truth is it's the best way to look at your relationship from a new perspective. We have to understand that there really isn't a "How to get through life" manual that comes with being human. As men, it's okay not to know everything. Doing workshops simply allows us to see some areas where we may be able to improve our lives. As I mentioned in the previous chapter, we literally spend billions of dollars on exterior things to try and create happiness, but it isn't until we go inside that we really make the positive dramatic shifts in our lives.

So maybe you're a little paranoid about workshops. Another thing you can do is simply educate yourself by reading books. Obviously you are committed to personal growth or you wouldn't be reading this book, so take a moment and acknowledge yourself for taking a step in the right direction. **Do it right now!** Tell yourself that you are committed to personal growth and creating great relationships, and you will create the type relationships that you truly deserve. When we make a habit of affirming things to ourselves, it's truly amazing how our lives shift for the better. A couple of really good books on the subject of relationships are: *How to Heal a Painful Relationship* by Bill Ferguson and *A Return To Love* by Marianne Williamson.

There are literally hundreds of great authors out there that share valuable insight and information that can assist us in transforming our relationships. We simply have to make sure that we are looking for the information.

Here's a simple exercise:

Relationships

Pick a time when you and your mate can have some quiet time alone together. Make a commitment to each other to be sincere and honest. Get a couple of sheets of paper. Each person gets a sheet and makes a list of ten things they like about the other person. Take some time and think about this. These ten things can be anything as long as it's something you like or admire about your mate. Once each of you has finished, exchange the list and go over them silently for a few minutes. After you've taken some time to let it all soak in, acknowledge your partner in whatever way you feel comfortable. A hug would be great, but a big sloppy passionate kiss will probably make the experience a lot more intimate. Commit to doing this five days in a row. Set aside a time that you won't be disturbed. If you need to get a babysitter, do so. If you miss a day, start all over. Make sure you do it five consecutive days; each day coming up with a different list. Once you make it to the fifth day, make arrangements to do something special together away from the house. Go out to eat or better yet go parking. That's right go parking and suck on each others face for awhile. Act like kids again, you deserve it. Sucking on each others face can be a joyful experience. Continue to make special time for you and your mate. We've become so busy in this society, we've lost touch with what's really important. As I've mentioned, we must create strong relationships in order to create strong families. I realize that a lot of you guys out there are still having the real-men-don't do-that conversation, but I assure you, they do. Not only that, I'm sure there was a time in your life when you did too. Were you a "real man" then?

It's really limitless as to what you can do to improve your relationships. It's simply a matter of choice. Will you choose to create great relationships? Or will you continue to pretend that you are fulfilling your male duty by not allowing a woman to love you the way you should? Playing that tired old game of "The Black Book Syndrome" which is accumulating all these phone numbers to prove your manhood. But the truth is, you're just like I used to be, scared to death that a woman could actually love you just the way you are. So stop pretending and get committed to creating meaningful, passionate relationships to last a lifetime. I promise, you will be a lot happier.

So what about the guys who are only contemplating a relationship right now? I want to share some things that might help you in locating that perfect someone.

When we start looking for that significant other, we need to know what it is that we are actually looking for. I was twenty one when I first got married, and the truth was, I didn't have a clue as to what qualities and values I was looking for in a woman. As a matter of fact I didn't even have a clue as to what values really were.

So my suggestion is the first thing you need to decide is what's really important to you. What are your values and beliefs that you would like to have in your mate? Take a moment and write down ten things that are really important to you and you wouldn't want to compromise them in a relationship.

Here's an example:

1. Spiritual
2. Attractive
3. Intelligent
4. Loving
5. Honest
6. Sexy
7. Active
8. Supportive
9. Ambition
10. Humorous

Once you've made your list based on what's important to you, then number them in order of importance. (Make sure you give this some careful consideration.) For example: If "sexy" is the most important thing to you on your list, put a number one next to "sexy." Then, if "intelligent" is number two, then put a number two by it. Continue until you complete all ten. Once you finish ask yourself: "Am I being totally honest with myself?" Are these the real qualities and values that are most important to me? If your list doesn't feel right, rewrite it. As a matter of fact, it may take some time just to develop the list. Take whatever time you need until you get it just right. You now have a great starting point to begin your quest for that special someone. The key is knowing what you're looking for and not compromising your values. I believe the reason a large majority of relationships don't work is simply because we really don't know ourselves and what we're looking for. When I first got married I didn't know these things. I was stuck on this societal roller coaster that said I was supposed to be married, so that's what I did. I hope you won't make the same mistake.

I would like to share with you an example of what happens when you choose to compromise your values in relationships.

Imagine that you are introduced to a co-worker or your best friend sets you up on a blind date. Of course the first thing we do as males is check out the package. In the beginning we're not interested in what's in the box, we're more interested in how the package looks on the outside. So you've met and you definitely like the packaging; everything is nice and pretty and put together just right. As a matter of fact, you wouldn't mind seeing this package underneath your Christmas tree. So she checks you out and decides that your packaging isn't too bad either, and maybe there is a chance that you will be under her tree as well.

So the initial attraction is established and you decide to go on a date. Being the gentleman that you are, you inform her that you will pick her up at eight, and she should be prepared to have the time of her life. Before you pick her up, you have to make sure that your package is wrapped perfectly. As a matter of fact, you go out and buy yourself some brand new wrappings. Of course, you also have to make sure that your package gives off a specific aroma that will catch her attention in case she doesn't notice the new wrappings. (Better safe than sorry, they always say.) So you're all wrapped up perfectly, and you arrive to pick up your date. You notice that she decided to put a little extra effort in wrapping her package, because you really didn't notice all those curves the first time. So you've got this huge grin on your face, and you just know that you have really got it going on. You get to dinner and you start the conversation with how nicely her package looks. If you're lucky she responds with the same compliment.

As the night progresses the conversation now shifts, and you start to get a few hints about what's really in the box. Unfortunately, as men, we usually disregard the contents because

Relationships

we're so mesmerized by the package. If we would simply learn to listen then we would recognize early that the contents of this particular package, sounds as if something might be broken. For example; she keeps talking about how all men are dogs, and how often she's been hurt and mistreated. She even says she doesn't trust men, but we simply refuse to get the message because we are still mesmerized by the packaging. Then we try and convince her that we're different and we aren't dogs. (Which some of us aren't.) We spend the entire evening trying to prove to her how nice we are and we're doing everything we can to get a chance to see her again. Hopefully we will have the opportunity to unwrap her packaging.

So, she buys your story and decides she wants to see you again. As usual the packaging is always wrapped just right, and you can't believe how lucky you are to have grabbed on to such a beautiful package. You walk around with your chest stuck out and take every opportunity to make sure all your friends see the beautiful package that you now get to call "Yours." The sad part is, you are completely oblivious to the fact that the contents of your package are definitely defective. After a month or so you notice little things that you should have noticed from the very beginning. For example, you never really noticed her vulgar language before; and you notice that the guy she said was just her friend certainly seems to be closer to her than you are because she's always mentioning his name. Then you notice that her conversation is limited to mono syllabic words, and she doesn't have a clue as to who Bill Clinton is. And there you are, dumbfounded, and asking yourself what happened to your wonderful lady.

The truth is, she was never wonderful to began with. You were so blinded by the beauty of the package and the wrappings you never really took the time to really find out what was in the box. If you would have established a clear set of values and refused to compromise them, you would have noticed on the very first date. But by not knowing what you were looking for from the beginning, you became involved with someone you really didn't want in the first place.

Now you're sitting at home, talking about how all women mistreat you simply because you didn't know what you were looking for in the first place. (For all the women out there, it's a simple story to illustrate a point. To get your lesson, simply do a role reversal of the characters. Don't accuse me of stereotyping all women.)

The point of that story is simple. We need to know what we're looking for, and we need to realize that the true person is on the inside. Living in an externally based society, we always seem to put the emphasis on what we see. But it's the qualities within a person that really makes the difference. So take some time and really get to know the person before you try and unwrap her package. I promise, it will save you a lot of time and effort.

Once you establish your list, don't compromise or you're headed for trouble. If you are a sexual dynamo and sex is high on your list, why get involved with Miss Goodie Twoshoes. Find yourself a super freak and get busy. Don't lie to yourself and say that you want to marry a really nice girl so mom will be proud of you. Be honest and know what you want. Don't concern yourself with what other people think about you. Satisfy your own needs. If you're a health enthusiast and are committed to health and fitness, how much sense does it make to get involved with someone who says she hasn't broken a sweat since she was twelve? If you have a Ph.D. and love intellectual stimulation, why become involved with someone who can't even spell "intelligence?" You get the point? Decide what's important to you and don't compromise. Oftentimes we go into relationships thinking that the other person will change to fit our needs. That is seldom the case. Never try to change anyone or allow them to change you. Know yourself and know what you want. Relationships will take on a whole new dynamic.

So for all you guys who don't have that special someone just yet, what have you been doing to attract that special someone? Are you still hanging out at bars looking for that one night stand? Or maybe you're waiting for that special someone to fall out of the sky? There are several things you can do to bring that wonderful woman into your life. This will probably make some of you a little uneasy, but have you considered running a personal ad? After all, now that you are clear on what you're looking for, you can use this as an opportunity to attract that number ten person into your life. Writing ads also gives you the opportunity to go over your values and qualities list. When you can create an ad and relay what you are looking for in a relationship through your words, you are definitely way ahead of the game. I assure you that most people can't write a personal ad because they honestly don't know what they are looking for. (Aren't you glad that you bought this book, with all it's valuable insight?)

I was very uncomfortable with the idea at first. Initially I felt as if I appeared desperate for a date. But I realize it's a very effective way to meet people. Of course, it doesn't always work, but it is a good lesson to experience. What the hell. Try it. You might like it.

Another option is a dating service. Although I haven't tried this one, I have gone to interview with several of the companies. If you have the money and are committed to creating a relationship, I see absolutely nothing wrong with this method. As a matter of fact it's probably the most intelligent. Just do some homework, because some of them are definitely overpriced.

Imagine that you've done your homework, and you've even decided to do some inner work. You're feeling great about yourself, and have established your hierarchy list of values. You are ready to create that loving relationship that you deserve. All of a sudden you meet the most incredible woman you've ever met. You check your list and she fits all the criteria for your soul mate, then you notice something about her that isn't on your list. Her skin color is different than yours. Now what? I believe that if you have taken the time to get to know yourself and what you're really looking for, what difference does color make? Remember what I said about the qualities are all on the inside? If this person has all that inside, then that's what's really important. On the other hand if you are specifically looking for someone of another color you had better check inside yourself and see what's going on. But ultimately, it's your decision. Take some time and consider the situation and if she really has all the qualities that you are looking for, then the two of you should be able to weather any storm. But be fully prepared, because it could be a rough ride. On the other hand it could be the smoothest ride you've ever taken. Good Luck!

So take a moment and visualize what the perfect relationship would be like.

Think about the wonderful feeling of unconditional love.

Relationships

Think about that significant other that is on your team supporting you with your dreams.
Think about incredible lovemaking beyond physical sex, deep passionate intimate en counters with the one you love.
Think about the wonderful family, filled with togetherness and warmth.
Think about that Soul-Mate that you become one with.
Think about the freedom and serenity that comes from knowing that your mates loves you and only you.
Think about a spiritual union between two people that can never be broken.
Think about that wonderful person that understands your fears and empowers you past any obstacle.
Think about being in love at the deepest level possible and having that love reciprocated back to you.
Think about Heaven on earth.
Think about a relationship filled with passion, love, honesty, trust, support, intimacy, peace, happiness' togetherness and joy.

Get those pictures in your mind and ask yourself how it would feel to have all of that in a relationship. Wouldn't it be wonderful? You're darn right it would! Is it really possible? Absolutely. Unequivocally. Yes!

As I mentioned earlier, I found my Soul-Mate. If I can do it, so can you.

Now that you have some insight into creating great romantic relationships, I would like to share with you how I found my Soul-Mate. After I addressed my issues and found the reasons why my first marriage didn't work out, I decided that I really did want to be married. Because of the new insights I gained, I felt confident that I could create a healthy, fulfilling relationship. During this time a friend of mine suggested that I read a book titled, *A Bridge Across Forever*. It is a wonderful story of a man who decided he wanted to create a love affair that would last forever.

It was in this book that I was first introduced to the concept of Soul-Mates. After completing the book, I knew that I wanted to find that one person that I could become one with. So the first thing I did was create a picture in my mind of what the perfect woman for me would be like. Following the guidelines that I talked about throughout this chapter, I wrote down exactly what I wanted my Soul-Mate to be like.

Here is what I wrote:

Soul-Mate

My Soul-Mate will be intelligent, physically fit, spiritual
and complete within herself.
She will be able to receive all the love I have to give
and also able to give her love freely.
She will be confident and centered and able to allow me the freedom
to be who I am, and I will do the same.
My Soul-Mate will be emotionally honest and trustworthy
and willing to become one with her spiritual equal.
Together we will grow and expand and
support each other in becoming all we were created to be.
She will have a great sense of humor
and we will spend hours just laughing and giggling and being silly.
We will take life sincerely, but not seriously.
She will love children and accept my children as her own.
We will vow to make our relationship a commitment to God
and therefore create a bond that can never be broken.
Everyday will be an acknowledgment of
how fortunate we are to have each other
and we will be committed to growing our relationship through eternity.
We will experience lovemaking at the deepest most intimate level possible,
and each encounter will be an expression of our deep love for one another.
We will travel the world together and
experience all the wonders of God's great creation called earth.
It will be the joining of two complete souls coming together to unite
in the love of God!

Saturday, 5/15/93
8:06 pm
MICHAEL

This was the vision I had for the woman I wanted to spend the rest of my life with. I read this vision everyday and I knew without question that one day I would find her. After a year and a half and over 17 different relationships, I still hadn't found her. My friends said that I was asking for too much and I would never find this dream woman. A lot of them said I was using this vision as an excuse to not be involved in a relationship. But I knew in my heart that she was out there, I simply had to be patient. Then one day I was walking through a grocery store and I heard someone say "Nice moustache!" Although I didn't see this person's face something told me to follow her and see if she was actually making a pass at me. After following her for a couple of aisles, I approached her and asked if she was speaking to me.

She said, "Yes," and I thanked her for the compliment. After a brief conversation, I asked for her phone number and asked if we might have a chance to get together sometime. She smiled and said, "The ball is in your court now."

I would love to give you all the details, but I'm saving them for an upcoming book that she and I are planning to write in the very near future. But to sum it all up, this wonderful woman that I met in the grocery store turned out to be the woman of my dreams. Without question, she is the woman that I plan to spend the rest of my life with, and I can't put words on the love and joy I feel by knowing that. In case you didn't notice, she is that beautiful woman posing with me on the back cover. Her name is Renee and she is everything that I dreamed of and more. So you simply must believe that you can find your Soul-Mate and be willing to do whatever it takes to find her (or him). Good Luck!

For this is the journey that men make to find themselves;
If they fail in this, it does not matter much what they find.
Money, Position, Fame, Many Loves, Revenge are all of little consequence.
When the tickets are collected at the end of the ride, they are all tossed in the bin marked "FAILURE".

But if a man happens to find himself;
If he knows what he can be depended on to do,
the limits of his courage,
the position from which he will no longer retreat,
the degree to which he can surrender his inner-life to some woman,
the secret reservoirs of his determination,
the extent of his dedication, the depth of his feeling for beauty,
his honest and unpostured goals-
Then he has found a mansion which he can inhabit with dignity all the days of his life.

James Michener

SEX AND MANHOOD

Can we talk? I mean can we really talk?

I realize we're about to enter into the area that every man thinks he's an expert, but the truth is most of us haven't a clue about the complexities associated with sex. We pretend that we're experts and always profess to being skilled, but deep down I think we're all somewhat confused. The good news is we don't have to know everything, but understanding some fundamentals can really alleviate some anxiety. I want you to remember, I am not an "Expert." I simply will share with you the lessons I've learned that have taught me to appreciate healthy sexuality. As you read this chapter, simply take the things that are applicable to you and use them. If you don't agree, that's all right, just make sure that you're being totally honest with yourself. I promise I will do the same.

Since the beginning of time manhood has been gauged by sexual conquest. If you look back in Greek mythology, you will find penis gods that were used to symbolize male power. In the early 1500's kings were known to have sexual liaisons with servants and the queens accepted it as part of the king's royal duties. In certain cultures polygamy is socially accepted as a religious rite, which entitles men to have more than one sexual partner. If you've happened to watch television within the last hour, I can guarantee that you have seen some advertisement with some pretty explicit sexual overtones. We are constantly bombarded with images of nudity and sex, yet I believe the vast majority of us are in the dark. I believe there are basically three reasons for this confusion:

First, because of the proliferation of all these sexual images, most of us haven't decided what's appropriate and what isn't. For example: as we watch the images on the screen we start to question if that's the way it's supposed to be done. Should I be prepared to engage in a sexual act with every female that I come into contact with? This is what society throws at us on a constant basis. Watch any soap opera and you will notice that sex is always an easy process without any complications.

Male sees female; female sees male; male becomes interested in female and makes his move; female is definitely interested so she responds positively. Male initiates process by kissing first; female finds the process stimulating, so she begins heavy breathing. Male takes this as clue that the process should continue and starts undressing female; female is now thoroughly involved in process. Once clothes are removed male and female engage in passionate lovemaking session in which they reach this simultaneous climax. The earth moves, there are screams of delight, and then it's over. Perfect! No hassles, no problems. Wouldn't it be nice if it were always that easy.

Secondly, a lot of us have hang-ups because of our upbringing. If we were taught as kids that sex was a dirty thing, then some of us carry that belief into our adulthood.

I think most males are brought up believing they're simply supposed to sleep with as many women as possible. (I remember my dad nudging me one day and asking me if I was getting any yet. I was only thirteen.) Our hang-ups as males usually center around performance anxiety and the lack of sex; whereas female hang-ups are being afraid to be labeled promiscuous. So they're usually trying not to give it away as much as we're trying to get it.

Thirdly, we have the religious beliefs. This plays a significant part in developing healthy sexuality. How can a person really enjoy something when they think God is watching and is going to punish them for their participation in this sinful act. (I'm really glad I didn't have to deal with that one.)

So we have the media telling us one thing, then our parents telling us something else. (Actually, most parents don't say anything directly. That's why we get most of our information from television.) And finally, we've got God looking over our shoulder. No wonder we're so confused.

So I am going to make an honest attempt to remove some confusion.

So let's start at the beginning. How many of you remember male "penis envy?" You know what I'm talking about — the time in junior high when you had to take a shower with a bunch of other guys and, for the first time in your life, you were exposed to a penis other than your own. You wanted to know if you measured up. Of course you couldn't go around just looking at other penises because then you would be accused of being gay, and that was the ultimate blow to the male ego. What you normally would do is stare at the ceiling, and run in and out of the shower as quickly as possible, then while you were drying off you could sort of sneak a peak. After the first few weeks, you were really concerned that yours wasn't quite as "progressed" as some of your other classmates and you were afraid that you would get the label "pencil dick." And there was always at least one guy who was well endowed and he would be the one who would make fun of everyone else. Occasionally he would totally humiliate someone by grabbing them and making fun of how small their penis was in comparison to his. Then everyone would jump in and laugh, and the poor unfortunate soul who got humiliated would be scarred for life because of the antics of Mr. Moosedick. And although we knew we couldn't measure up to King Dong we usually looked up to him as some sort of god. That is the origin of penis envy. If you take some time and look back in retrospect, I'm sure you will agree with me. Not only was it unfair, but it was a pretty stressful situation to be in. Do you remember sitting in the bath tub just staring at the darn thing and wondering when it was really going to grow?

Then all of a sudden the darn thing got a mind of its own. For no apparent reason it would jump to attention and cause you considerable embarrassment. It seemed as though you didn't have any control over it what-so-ever. You'd be in history class, and the teacher would call you to the front of the room to work on a problem, then all of a sudden you had this rock hard erection. The first thing you would do is stick your hand in your pocket and try to calm it down. But that only made it worse. Touching it seemed to stimulate it even more. Then you might try the old, hide-it-behind-a-book trick. But that didn't work if you didn't have a book.

If you were lucky you got in front of the class unnoticed and continued to face the blackboard until the erection subsided. Then after school you'd have this long conversation with mister penis: "Why did you embarrass me like that? What's gotten into you lately? First you wake me up early in the morning, and sometimes you wake me up in the middle of the night spitting this icky stuff out. I don't know what to do with you any more." So you're thirteen years old, your penis is out of control, and you have no one to talk to.

Wasn't puberty a trip? If only some one would have sat you down and explained everything to you, life would have been a lot simpler, don't you agree?

So as we look back, we can see how we become so obsessed with this whole sexuality issue. No one ever explained anything to us so, we're left out in the dark to try and figure it out on our own. So what is the next step we normally take? Since our parents won't talk to us, then whose the next person in line that we go to for help? Our friends! This is usually our biggest mistake. First of all, they usually know less than we do, but they won't admit that. Secondly, they usually lie to us.

Of course, as males, we have perfected lying as a work of art when it comes to sex. Even at a very young age we learn how to never seem inadequate at this thing called sex. I was reading Bill Cosby's book "Childhood" and he talked about this lying phenomenon. He talked about a conversation he and a friend had concerning "Getting some 'Jones.'" (I had never heard the term before but it was simply one of the many metaphors we create to discuss sex.) In this conversation his friend asked him if he was getting any Jones. Although he had no idea what Jones meant, he didn't want to be considered a square, so he automatically responded, "Of course I'm getting some, what about you? "

"Man, I get it all the time," his friend replied. "So, how do you do it?" he asks.

"Oh, the regular way, you know what I mean."

"Yea, the regular way. That's the way I like to do it too."

I know you remember that same conversation, don't you?

We get through junior high realizing that this thing is loaded, but we still haven't figured out what to do with it. Then we start to put two and two together, and we have our first sexual revelation. Females! That's what this darn thing is for. We've seen the male and female together on television, but somehow it didn't compute. In junior high, females were used to punch on and play cooties with, and although you've pretended to know everything about sex, you never really considered that this penis was somehow to be used to attract females. Paydirt! Now you've got it figured out.

So you get to high school, and now the conversation is a little different. You're not as concerned about the size of your penis anymore. The question now becomes: Where are you going to put it? Females take on a whole new role in high school. All of a sudden you're concerned about how you look; the clothes you wear, the type of hairstyle you have, how big your muscles are, and things like this. Why? Because you're trying to attract females.

So why are you trying to attract females? Because you have come to the conclusion that that's where mister penis belongs. And how did you decide on this? By watching television and listening to your friends.

So you're cruising through high school and you meet you're high school sweetheart. (If you're lucky.) Everything is going smoothly. You gathered up enough courage to finally kiss her. You've made it to first base! Then you become a real man because, for the first time in your life, you've made contact with a breast other than your mom's. You've gained a lot of confidence and have made it to second. So you go to a high school dance and get the opportunity "to grind" for the first time. And now you're rounding third. After a couple of beers, you lower your head and dash for home. You're going at full throttle and the only concern is touching home plate. Within an instant (literally), you've scored. You stop, scratch your head and ask "Scored what?" You remember passing second, and have a glimpse of what third was like, but now everything's a blur. You've reached home plate, but something's missing.

Where's the trophy? Don't I get something? I wonder if I did something wrong? That was quick. It didn't look that way on television. Is that all there is? You mean I got all worked up for this thing called sex and this is it? I think I'll go play basketball.

Take a moment and think about your first experiences with sex. What are some of the messages you received? What do you remember? As children we received lots of different messages about sex, but unfortunately most of them weren't very accurate. You have to be willing to look at the origin of your sexual behavior if you're going to develop healthy sexuality. Starting at the beginning is best. If you choose to participate in some inner-child work, it will identify a lot of your behaviors and the root causes of them.

In her book *Love, Sex, Death, and the Making of the Male*, Dr. Rosalind Miles did in-depth research into the origins of male behavior. She researched history, psychology, literature and science and came to the conclusion that this phenomenon of sexual conquest is deeply rooted within our society. She coined a term "Phallocentricity" which is difficult to say, but translates to "thinking with the little head instead of the big one." It is this phenomenon that causes so much pain and destruction in our lives, as far as men are concerned.

Let's take a look at this process called "phallocentricity." As I've mentioned, the media plays a very important part in shaping our beliefs, especially in the area of sexuality. We are constantly bombarded with images and messages that can and do have negative impact on our belief systems. Take a moment and think about not only the images, but the sounds as well. I did a random survey of songs on a local black radio station and it's no wonder our kids are as confused about sex as we are. Here's a few examples of what I heard: One guy was begging his girlfriend to let him lick her up and down. Then there was the female that was professing to like all types of penises, she didn't care if they were hard or soft, short or long. Another guy was singing about hitting a "G" spot. (Let your imagination figure that one out.) And one of them actually imitated a female reaching orgasm. Now in no way am I a prude, but how can we expect our children to behave any other way. We have got to understand that the media has a powerful influence on the way we interact with each other in any social situation. But the one thing we don't want to do is place the entire blame on the media. I believe that the media does an extremely irresponsible job of portraying the news, yet I have to take responsibility for my own actions. I hope you do the same.

So let's take a look at some of the myths and beliefs about black males.

If you go back a few years, you will probably remember the role models we had as males. Do you remember Superfly, Black Caesar, The Mack, and Shaft? As a matter of fact, my nickname throughout my junior high years was Superfly. In case you don't remember, these guys were all tough cops, pushers or pimps. In each case they were nonemotional and always had more than one woman. Whenever they would interact with females, it was usually in a violent manner. You never saw the guy holding his woman tenderly and expressing to her how much she meant to him. It was usually "Hey, bitch, how much money did you make me?" or maybe "Come here winch and give me some pussy." Without question those negative images had an effect on our male psyche. So now we move into the nineties, and although the images have made a turn towards more positive role models, we're still inundated with negative images. It truly amazes me that so many of our new black directors are still portraying us the way we've been trying to get away from for years. I personally would love to see a movie filled with black males that are emotionally secure, and a story about black males and relationships without the vulgarity and violence. (Maybe I'll write a story and produce my own movie. Hmmm, I feel that creative energy moving already.) The point I'm trying to make is, sometimes we create beliefs based on those negative images. And if we don't interrupt those negative beliefs, we will keep acting out in the negative manner.

So here are some beliefs that some of us hold on to that usually cause a lot of problems in our sexual interactions:

1. ALL MEN THINK ABOUT IS SEX.

I read a statistic once that said some men think about sex sixty percent of the time. For the most part I think most statistics are useless, but this makes a great topic for discussion. I tried to be totally honest with myself and wanted to see how much time I spent thinking about sex. I came to the conclusion that if I thought about sex more than ten percent of the time, I'd be surprised. As a matter of fact, I think that's a pretty high figure for me. Maybe my libido is a little slow. How about you? Do you spend the majority of your day in fantasy land with bodacious babes? I think that's a myth. I guess there are several variables to consider: age, marital status and more, but I think that's pretty ridiculous. If you think men are bad, you need to take a look at some of the covers of women's magazines. I think they're thinking about it a lot more than we are. You would think that if everyone's thinking about it, and apparently doing it, it must be a pleasurable experience. But my question is why is everyone so dissatisfied? Keep reading, I may answer that question.

2. MEN ARE ALWAYS READY TO HAVE SEX.

Here's one that creates lots of anxiety, whether you will admit it or not. As I've mentioned before, we are constantly bombarded with images that show men as always ready, willing, and able to have sex. I heard in a movie once that "Men don't need a reason for sex, they simply need a place." A lot of us try and act that out. Let's see if this conversation sounds familiar: you're at the beach with a couple of your friends. All of a sudden this perfect ten body walks by. Immediately the male ego kicks in.

Brother #1. Man, if I had that I'd bang the shit out of her.
Brother #2. That woman is so fine, I'd like to just jump her bones right here and right now.
Brother #3. Neither one of you would know what to do with that.
You'd better let a real man handle this.

Of course we all know this conversation, don't we?

But the truth is, if she came up to either one of the brothers, right there on the beach, dropped her bikini, and said, "Here it is. Take it." What do you think would happen? I realize some of you macho men out there are saying "Boy I'd wear her out." But the truth is, the vast majority of us wouldn't know what to do. Of course, this is a hypothetical situation. But ask yourself honestly, what would you do? I'm not asking you to think about the risk factors involved, like AIDS and other diseases; I'm simply asking if we are always ready to have sex, are we able to perform on a moments notice? I will assert that we aren't. Let's evaluate this scenario. First of all the environment is definitely not conducive to great sex. You're out in the open amongst strangers, and, more importantly, your friends. Here's a woman that you don't know anything about, and she comes and throws her stuff in your face. (Who knows where it's been or what's been in it.) It's probably 100 degrees (or hotter), and there's sand on everything, not to mention you didn't even have any condoms. So are you really ready?

We, as men, have been conditioned to believe that sex is an easy process, and we should always be prepared to do it. The truth is, it's never that easy. As a matter of fact, the first time you sleep with anyone it's usually a pretty uncomfortable situation.

So now that we have that door open, let's walk through it.

The one thing that we as males never discuss is impotence. You know what that is, right? If not, it's when mister penis decides he doesn't want to cooperate. You need to realize that impotence is just as natural as breathing, and whether you admit it or not, it's happened to you. Ask yourself if you relate to this. You meet this wonderful woman, make your move and get her into bed. At first everything is great. Mister penis is hard as a rock and you're ready to get busy. There's a lot of heavy breathing and now you've just about got all your clothes off. All of a sudden you realize mister penis has went to sleep. Now, you panic. You realize that this woman is waiting for you, but she doesn't know that mister penis is taking a nap. The harder you try to wake mister penis up, the deeper he goes into his sleep. Now ask yourself: "Who's in control here, you or mister penis?" It appears that mister penis has the upper hand,

Sex and Manhood

but the truth is, you're the one that controls mister penis. The reason mister penis has gone to sleep is because you've put too much pressure on him too quickly, and tried to force him to do something he really wasn't ready to do. Its called "performance anxiety." And when mister penis decides he wants to shut down because you're trying too hard, he'll do just that. Now you really start to panic. The woman is moaning and groaning, and your manhood is on the line. What next? You say you're a little tense, and maybe you just need to lay down for a minute, but, in your mind, you're so mad at mister penis for letting you down, you could ring his neck. But that wouldn't be a very smart move, would it? By being angry at mister penis, it only makes the situation worse. As a matter of fact, mister penis loves humiliating you because you usually treat him poorly by expecting to much from him. Always trying to get him to be at your beck and call, putting him in places he really doesn't want to be and wearing those damn tight jeans that cut off his circulation. So now he has the opportunity to laugh at you, and, I promise, he's really getting a kick out of seeing you squirm.

So, maybe you decide to go get a beer to relax you a little. Big mistake! Alcohol is a depressant. It only slows things down, and the last thing mister penis needs is to be intoxicated. So, now you're really pissed. The woman is no longer interested, and mister penis has won. The result is a shattered ego, that's all. It's really not the end of the world. But to us it's the ultimate humiliation. Why? Because we're conditioned to believe that we're always supposed to be ready to have sex.

To alleviate some pressure, I'll share a secret with you. You know what's the best thing to do when you're in that situation? It's really simple. Talk to your mate! Tell her that mister penis is making things difficult, and you realize he's trying to tell you something. Maybe he's tired, or maybe you're pushing him too hard. It could be that the medication you took is having an effect on him. It could be that mister penis is sick and needs some medical assistance. If you open the line of communication, I promise mister penis will respond in a positive way. Don't get angry and think that you're going to get even. If you do, you're doomed. Mister penis will win every time. Your best bet is to make friends with him, and develop a healthy relationship with yourself, from a sexual perspective that is.

We really put a lot of pressure on ourselves when it comes to sex. The truth is, we need to take some time and develop healthy sexual attitudes about ourselves and our bodies. There really isn't an owners manual that comes with our sexual organs, but if we decide to investigate just a little, we can really create open communication with ourselves and our mates. So, remember, every male has experienced this, you are definitely not alone. Make friends with mister penis, and he'll make friends with you.

For all you super studs out there who are sticking your chest out because you know what a great lover you are, let me burst your bubble. Remember the Richard Pryor joke about sexual performance? You don't? Well, let me remind you: Richard was obviously involved in an argument with his girlfriend about sex. He was bragging about his sexual proficiency and the conversation went something like this.

Richard: "I'm really tired of your old p---y, I'm going to go out and find me some new p---y"
Girlfriend: "Well if you had two more inches of d--k ,you'd find some new p---y here"
Richard: (obviously shocked) "What do you mean? You know this d--k is good to you. If it weren't good, then why were you hollering?"
(I bet he had his chest stuck out at this point.)
Girlfriend: "I was hollering to keep from laughing in your face!"

Ouch! The ultimate blow to the male ego. I'm sure all he could do at this point was pick his face up off the ground and leave. I doubt if he wanted to have sex with her after that exchange. The point is, all this time we as men have been trying to get our strokes by being great sexual partners, and a large percentage of the time we weren't doing nearly as well as we thought. Need I remind you of the percentages of women that say they fake orgasms? In case you haven't heard, the term for someone who is constantly trying to prove his manhood by sexual conquest is "Sex Addict." I hope you don't fit into that category. So, rather than be Mister Bang-Your-Brains-Out, why not focus on deep, intimate, caring, sexual encounters with someone you really care about. When you develop that level of intimacy and trust, there is absolutely no way you can't have great sex.

3. BLACK MEN ARE ALL HUNG TO THEIR KNEES

Remember penis envy? This is the reason it exists. This is definitely a societal stereotype. If you will look at the images, what do you see? Brothers walking around grabbing their crotches and always using that penis as the pinnacle of power. So let's be honest. Although I didn't do any formal survey on this topic, I think it's safe to assume that there isn't validity to this myth. As human beings, we come in all shapes, colors and sizes, and I'm sure that is the case with mister penis. So whatever you were blessed with, I suggest you be happy with it. Remember, mister penis is your friend or he can be your worst enemy. It's your choice. Don't be all hung up with size. Remember: "It's not the size of the ship, but the motion of the ocean that makes the difference."

4. THE EIGHT HOUR ORGASM

I remember listening to a Richard Pryor album about this particular topic. He said "How many of you have heard brothers say they have eight hour orgasms? I want you to know that they're lying! I personally have one minute orgasms then I need eight hours of sleep!" Here's another one of those myths that can cause a lot of anxiety. The truth is, there isn't a way to gauge how long you're supposed to last. If you're all wrapped up into performance, you're going to miss the best part. Just relax and enjoy the moment. I promise the more you relax, the longer it will last.

I think that sums it up. If you will take some time to develop some healthy sexual attitudes about yourself, sex will take on a whole new meaning. The key is openness and honesty. If you allow yourself to communicate openly with your mate, you can create a level of intimacy that will guarantee great sex. The secret to remember is you actually make love to your woman in your mind, not through mister penis. When you develop that love affair on a deep emotional and spiritual level, there is absolutely no way you can't make love forever.

Let's take an honest look at your approach to sexuality. Answer these questions honestly:

Are you still acting out the little black book mentality?

In case you're not sure what that is, let me elaborate:
Are you sexually involved with more than one woman?
When you're participating with your mate sexually, is your main focus to try and knock another hole in it?
Are you trying to bang the shit out of her?
Are you concerned about your mates sexual needs?
Are you comfortable buying condoms at the store?
Can you stand in front of the mirror totally nude and say "I Love My Body?"
Can you openly discuss your sexual needs with your mate?
Are you comfortable having sex with the lights on?
How much time do you honestly spend engaged in sexual intercourse. In most cases you'll find its a very small percentage.
Do you ever use sex as a means to "Get even" with your mate (withholding sex)?

Take a moment and just think about these questions. Sexuality has many facets. It's simply a matter of us being willing to look at it from a different perspective. I hope you will recognize the erroneous beliefs you may have had about sex. Hopefully you can make some changes that will enhance your sex life for the better.

So, now let's talk about manhood.

Remember the story "The Emperor's New Clothes?" It was the story where an emperor hired a tailor to make him some new clothes, and the tailor convinced him that only intelligent people could see them. Of course there were no clothes, but because the emperor didn't want to be labeled a fool, he pretended that he could see them. So the emperor is parading through town with his invisible clothes, and everyone knew he was naked, but no one had the courage to say anything. Finally this kid speaks out, and starts laughing. Then everyone else follows his lead.

That story is analogous to manhood in our society. Most of us have been parading around following society's definition of manhood and have been pretending that we really like it. We walk around thinking that we are hot stuff, when we have multiple sex partners. We overwork ourselves to the point of exhaustion, and rationalize it by saying we're successful. We go to "Happy Hour" and pretend that we're having a good time. We have heart attacks at age fifty and think it's normal. We talk about how much we care about our children, yet they never see us or spend time with us. We over-indulge in drugs and alcohol and say it's the only way to deal with the stress. And we blame the "System" for not giving us a fair break. All these habits are part of the male conditioning of our society. A large percentage of us are continuing to pretend that we are wearing "The Emperor's New Clothes"! But finally some of us have begun to speak out, and we are realizing that we have been walking around naked. This speaking out has been labeled the "Men's Movement," and I think it's the most positive thing that has happened in this country in a very long time.

The "Men's Movement" is about redefining what manhood really means. It's a cry for help from those of us who are tired of living the lie. The male role in society is changing very rapidly, and for those of us who choose to recognize this positive shift in male belief systems, we will experience life the way it is really meant to be. I'd like to touch on some of the key areas that this movement is addressing.

First, we are beginning to understand that our childhood sets the stage for how we participate in all of our interactions with other human beings. We are learning that our childhood beliefs are carried with us through our adulthood and if we have traumatic experiences during this time, it will carry through to our adult lives. If these issues aren't addressed, then it becomes virtually impossible to develop close, intimate relationships with other people. We are also recognizing that our relationship with our parents play a significant role in how we participate in relationships and how we raise our own children. I will discuss this in more detail in the next chapter.

Secondly, we are rethinking our position on careers and priorities. It is no longer acceptable to keep killing ourselves at a job we hate. The time has come when we reshift our priorities and understand that "Making it to the top" may not be in our best interest if it means we won't have time to enjoy our families and friends. We can still be successful, yet we learn to balance our lives.

Thirdly, it's time to make relationships top priority. Understanding that having a loving spouse and family is essential to success. Of course everyone's not going to be married, but I think it's time to start developing loving, intimate relationships that are rewarding and mutually fulfilling. It's time to eliminate these short term meaningless relationships. This means creating relationships based on trust, openness and honesty.

Fourth, we have to eliminate society's myths about how we interact sexually with our mates. As males, we must be able to communicate our sexual needs; we must start making love to our mates instead of just having sex with them. We must accept the fact that touching and caressing isn't a sign of weakness and focus on our mate's sexual needs as well as our own. We must eliminate the "wham-bam thank-you-ma'am" approach to sex. Creating deep, loving, sexual encounters with the women we love must be a priority.

Fifth, we must take care of our physical bodies. Understanding that "An ounce of prevention is worth a pound of cure."

Sixth, we must develop a spiritual connection with our creator. Whatever works for you. This is essential!

I think that sums it up. If we choose to incorporate these new beliefs systems, there is no way we can't put this country back on track. It's going to take a united effort, but it starts with the man in the mirror. Take a stand and be a real man!

Speak to us of Children

Your children are not your children.
They are the sons and daughters of Life's longing for itself.
They come through you, but not from you.
And though they are with you, they belong not to you.
You may give them your love, but not your thoughts
For they have their own thoughts.
You may house their bodies, but not their souls.
For their souls dwell in the house of tomorrow, which you can
      never visit, not even in your dreams.
You may strive to be like them, but seek not to make them like you.
For life goes not backward nor tarries with yesterday.
You are the bows from which your children as living
      arrows are sent forth.
The archer sees the mark upon the path of the infinite
      and he bends you with his might that His arrows
      may go swift and far.
Let your bending in the archers hand be for gladness;
For even as He loves the arrow that flies,
so He loves also the bow that is stable.

KAHLIL GIBRAN

CHILDREN

Without question, our children are our future.

If we aren't putting emphasis on our children's well-being now, what does the future hold? I realize that politicians have been using children as the basis of their campaigns, yet I believe that most of it is simply political rhetoric. The time has come that we, as males, take a more active role in our own children's lives. We must take responsibility for our children's success. As the preceding poem stated: "You are the bow which the archer uses to send his arrows into the world." My question is: "What direction are you sending your arrows?" As I've mentioned, the male role in society is changing dramatically. A lot of the old rules are no longer acceptable. Not participating in our children's well-being can no longer be tolerated.

As I look around and see all the unwed mothers trying to bring up their children alone, I realize that we have to do everything within our power to curb this very serious problem. If you've decided to take responsibility for your success, you must realize that if you have children they are a part of that success. We cannot afford to father children, then disappear from their lives. Our input as fathers is extremely important in the developmental stages of our children's self esteem. It is my belief that although mothers usually spend more time with the children than the fathers do, the fathers actually have a larger impact on the child's confidence and feelings of self-worth.

Because of the patriarchal structure of our culture, the male role had never included nurturing and parenting skills. As men, we have always carried the role of breadwinner and protector. We were always expected to provide shelter, food and discipline, and, in the case of our sons, we were expected to make sure that they were tough and non-emotional. These roles are definitely changing. As more women join the work force and take on their new roles in corporate America, we have to take on the new parenting roles within the home. Of course, most people fear change and it can be very uncomfortable at the beginning, but we have got to make the commitment to developing parental skills. As a father of three wonderful children, I can honestly say that it is without question one of the most rewarding, fulfilling experiences a man can have. Of course it's not for everyone, but for those of us who choose to do so, it can actually be the highlight of our lives. Very few things compare to the feeling I get when I hear my children telling their friends how cool and smart their dad is. I just swell up with pride inside and it let's me know that I'm doing a good job as a father.

So what I would like to do is share a few things I've learned, not only through my research but also through the participation with my own children. Hopefully you will pick up some insight on raising your children and then you can pass your skills on to them, and ultimately they will pass these skills on to their children and we will create a cycle of nurturing that will be passed on for generations.

First, we have to start with the pregnancy.

Not too long ago our roles as men was to simply plant the seed and let the women do the rest. We were not taught that our participation in these nine months were really important, so we basically watched as our wives went through all these hormonal and emotional changes. After nine months we would take them to the hospital, drop them off in the emergency room, then have a seat in the waiting room until our child was born. After a few hours (if our wives were lucky), the baby was born and they were placed in a room with lots of other babies. We would stand on the outside of the window and point out our newborn to anyone who happened to be within a fifty yard radius. We would sit out there and smile and feel so proud. We thought it was appropriate to celebrate, so we would go out and buy cigars to pass out to our friends. *Then* we would go see our wives, and although she looked as though she had just competed in the triathlon, we would say how beautiful she looked. After a day or two we took our newborn and exhausted wife home, and was welcomed with gifts and congratulations from family and friends. After a few months the newness wore off and, as men, we sort of slipped back into our old routine, and barely made time to spend with our new additions. Before we knew it, they were in school and growing like weeds. Pretty soon we don't even recognize them. With the exception of an occasional birthday party, a few disciplinarian conflicts, and some confrontations about grades, for the most part we missed the whole process of them growing up.

Now enter the 90's, we've come to understand the importance of emotional support during this very stressful time. Instead of just watching, we can now take Lamaze classes and actually understand what the hell is going on. We now realize that the reason our wives started crying uncontrollably when we said she burned the bacon has absolutely nothing to do with us. This major shift in her hormonal system is the cause, so now we don't have to feel as guilty. We also learned that honesty is not necessarily the best policy when our wives ask us if she looks fat. We have to compensate for this imbalance by being tactful. And that means stretching the truth just a little bit.

Once the baby decides it wants to see the world, we rush to the hospital, but this time we're well prepared. Not only are we allowed in the delivery room, but we can now go in armed with video cameras. (I personally would never do that, but it is definitely an option.) So, we must admit, times have definitely changed. Because of our new insight and closeness with our mates, we can now go in and tell our wives that they look like someone who just went a full fifteen rounds with Evander Holyfield.

My point is that we have got to make a more concerted effort in assisting our mates in this very stressful situation. We must also realize that this is a time of great stress for us also, and we must reach out to friends and family to support us during this time. We must understand that it's okay not to know everything, but we must make the effort to learn as much as possible. Discussing your fears and concerns about the upcoming addition to your family is a good way to help you adjust to the changes in your lifestyle. When we learn to understand that we do have fears and concerns that are normal, we can openly discuss these issues and thereby eliminate a lot of anxiety.

I remember when my former wife and I had our second child there were a lot of complications in the delivery. It was a very stressful situation. I honestly didn't know how to handle it emotionally, so I just numbed out. I simply chose not to experience the fear and sadness that I felt at the time. My inability to discuss this with anyone made the whole experience more difficult. By shutting down, it made my entire life miserable. I couldn't operate effectively at work and it actually distanced me from my mate because I was too afraid to talk about my fears. If you are in this situation, you *must* understand that the key is support. Find someone to talk to and don't keep everything bottled up inside. As soon as you decide to seek support, you will find that you aren't alone and most of your fears are unwarranted. As soon as we make the commitment to get involved, the entire process becomes easier for everyone.

Once we have experienced the joys and pains of childbirth, then we must make a commitment to being a significant part in that child's upbringing for life. No matter what happens, that child will always be a part of you. It's your responsibility to be there for that child.

As I've mentioned, I am not an expert, but I would like to share with you some lessons and knowledge I've gained over the years. So, after childbirth, we need to recognize that a child basically has four fundamental stages that are essential to its emotional and psychological well being.

Stage 1   Newborn: From birth to 18 months.

This is probably the most important stage of all. Remember the analogy of the computer? Well, your new computer is completely blank and it's just waiting for you to start programming in information. In the past we have left this stage to the mother, for the most part, we had never really participated in this important stage. But I assure you that your participation is extremely important. Of course most of us are extremely uncomfortable just trying to hold a newborn infant. Speaking from my own experience I was always afraid that I would hold the baby wrong and break its fragile little neck. Then of course there are those shitty diapers that were always filled with surprises. But the time has come when we are able to hold and nurture our children and create that bond that mothers have been creating for years.

I realize that most women do have that maternal instinct that makes this process a little easier to accept, but I also know that men can and do bond with their children if they will put forth the effort. So my recommendation is that you participate in that bonding process. Now there is no reason to become afraid. All that means is that you should spend as much time as possible holding and telling your child how glad you are to have him/her in your life. Hug your child as much as possible; kiss them and tell them how happy they make you feel. I realize this can be uncomfortable at first, especially if you've never done it before, but it will get easier with time, I promise. It is essential to that child's upbringing. Did you know that there have been studies that have shown that babies will actually die if they aren't held and nurtured? Touch is very important in the development of that child's entire neurological and emotional system. Another good idea is to play with your newborn, wiggle his or her fingers and toes. Make googlie noises and funny faces. Laugh with your child and develop a sense of humor towards the entire process. You will both benefit.

Buy educational toys and read child rearing books. Sing to your child and count your blessings for this incredible gift. Make it a point to spend as much time alone with your child as possible; take ownership of your creation. Make sure that you have the opportunity to feed your child also, it can be a great bonding experience. Most of all, thank your wife for the pain and suffering she endured to bring your child into the world. The best way to do that is by participating in your child's upbringing. I promise you, that is the best way to repay her.

Once you get the hang of bonding it's on to the next stage;

Stage 2   Infant: From 19 months to 36 months

This is where the real challenge begins. Unfortunately, we usually associate this stage with "the terrible twos," but the truth is, it is simply a stage of learning self-awareness and gaining personal power. This is when the child constantly says "No" to everything you tell them. In the past we have considered this negative behavior, but the truth is, the child is only trying to develop its own sense of self. Those outbursts are simply the child's way of saying "I am somebody!" Contrary to popular belief, the child is not just trying to drive you nuts. We must understand that a child at this age really doesn't have the capacity for cognitive thinking. He isn't being defiant on purpose; he's simply trying to find himself and figure out who he is. At this stage, it's the only way he can do this. I realize this may be hard to believe, but the truth is, this is the time when we must be most tolerant. One of the most destructive things we can do in this stage is not let the child express himself. We should never shame the child by screaming negative comments at him. We should take the time and try and answer all their questions because their little computer is absorbing a lot of information in a very short period of time. We must make sure that the information is positive, nurturing and beneficial to the child's self esteem. By allowing the child to ask questions and be inquisitive, we open the door for continued growth and a positive self-image.

Of course, this is the time when the child becomes mobile and wreaks havoc on all your belongings; so if you decide to have children make sure you prepare your residence to accommodate your child's curiousness. Whatever you do, please refrain from screaming at your child. Always realize that the child is like a sponge soaking up information, and all it really wants to do is learn about the world around it. Give them room to grow and learn. During this time you should make an extra effort to instill in your child a love for learning. Read to your child as often as possible; make sure you allow them to see you reading also. Kids always duplicate our actions, not our words, so please lead by example. Buy educational toys for your child and invest some time playing with your child. You don't have to give up your masculinity to play with your child. Have fun and be a kid yourself. It will do wonders to reduce your stress levels.

Stage 3   Adolescent: (Preteen) From 3 years to 12 years

This is the stage of developing self-responsibility. The child has developed a sense of self and now needs to be given tasks which will continue to increase his feelings of confidence. During this stage the child likes to do things on his own. And wants to be acknowledged for his accomplishments. He also starts breaking away from the parents and laying the foundations for their likes and dislikes. This is the period where the child likes to start collecting things and really becomes attached to objects. He starts accumulating things to create a sense of ownership within himself. He also starts developing relationships outside the family. These relationships become a very important part in his life. The peer group becomes a significant element in the child's decisions.

During this time it's extremely important to "mirror" the child. Which means to look the child in the eye and compliment him or her on their accomplishments. Giving positive feedback on the things done. This is extremely important. We sometimes neglect to acknowledge the things our kids do that are right, and put more focus on what they do wrong. This can be very detrimental to the child's self esteem. Please make an effort to focus on the positive rather than the negative. Take some time to visit your child's school and see the work that they do. Whenever there is a Father's Day activity, please participate. When your child sees that you have taken time out to come and see his work and his school environment, it will work miracles for self-esteem. I've had the opportunity to do this on occasion and I can't tell you how my children's eyes light up when they see me walk in the room. Your kids will really enjoy showing you off to their friends. I realize most of us have extremely busy schedules, but there is absolutely no reason why you shouldn't be able to attend a few functions within the span of a school year. If possible, take your kids to your job. Take some time and explain what you do. Allow them to ask questions about your job. Whatever you do, don't be ashamed of your job. Whether you believe it or not, your kids love you unconditionally. All they want to know is what their dad does. If for some reason you aren't satisfied with your position, take this as an opportunity to make some changes.

Make it a point to ask your child's opinions on different topics. Ask them lots of questions about their lives and what they enjoy doing. Ask them about their friends, and be sure the line of communication is always open. Make sure you take some time to hug your child, boy or girl. Although this may be uncomfortable at first, it's essential to the development of your child's psychological and emotional well-being. I realize that this is a stretch for most men. Unfortunately most of us never received hugs ourselves, and it may make you break out in a cold sweat. But, I promise you, that practice makes perfect. After a few times you will really start enjoying it yourself. Because of the homophobic culture we live in, most males see hugging and touching as a sign of weakness. But the truth is, it is definitely a sign of strength. When a man is secure enough in himself that he isn't concerned about what society or other people think about him, he will definitely experience levels of confidence within himself that will allow him to be and express all that he is. In doing so, he will develop closeness and intimacy at a level most men only wish they could attain. So forget the message that real men don't like to be touched. It's part of your nature and it feels great to do. Hugging your child is essential to your child's well-being.

Stage 4   Teenager: From 13 to19 years old

I think if we would simply take a moment and remember how awkward being a teenager was for us, we would be more compassionate with our teenagers. Being a teenager is definitely a stressful time for the child and us as well. Becoming a teenager means it's time to face the real world. It's the time when the child wants to be completely responsible for his own life. I believe that it is definitely much harder on teenagers now than it was twenty years ago. When the child becomes a teenager he simply creates the belief that he can make it on his own. It's the time when he actually is held accountable for his actions. I believe that if we, as fathers, develop a close relationship with our children early, this whole process would be a lot easier for everyone concerned. At this stage, a lot of kids will bond with groups outside of the family unit. It's a time when friends are extremely important, and the peer group plays a major factor in the child's decisions. It is an important time for the child to feel that he belongs to a group. It is my belief that the reason some of our youth are participating in gangs is simply because they are trying to connect with a group to receive the acceptance that they are not receiving at home. As fathers, we must provide the nurturing environment that our kids need at this critical time in their lives. If we don't, then we lose them to gangs and other negative influences. This has to be top priority in our lives. Whatever it takes, we must participate with our teenagers to keep them away from all the violent, negative situations they will definitely encounter.

One way to connect with your teen is by receiving a parental report card. I suggest that you allow your teen *to grade you on your job as a father*. Of course this will probably make both of you extremely uncomfortable, but it will allow you to see what kind of relationship you have established with your child. It's actually very simple:

First, you have to commit to being open-minded. If you are going to stay stuck in your self-righteousness and not be honest, this report card won't benefit anyone. But, on the other hand, if you sincerely want to create a open relationship with your child, this report card could change your relationship with your child dramatically.

Take a sheet of paper and draw up a report card using these ten criteria as your subjects,
1. Honesty
2. Open-mindedness
3. Participation in child's life
4. Keeps promises
5. Listening to child's problems
6. Has fun with child
7. Teaches child new things (read together or other activity)
8. Makes physical contact with child (Hugs)

9. Gives child positive encouraging affirmations.
10. Tells child that you love them and care about them.

Take these ten criteria and ask your child to grade you just like they are graded in school. "A" being the highest score, "F" being the lowest score. Tell your child that this is extremely important to you and you want him to be completely honest without fear of negative ramifications. (And make sure you mean that.) Give them the report card and allow them to spend some time thinking about what grades you should receive. Make sure you aren't around while they are scoring you. (We wouldn't want them to feel intimidated would we?) After you receive your grades take some time alone and simply accept the feedback. Don't get angry or discount their grades. Simply look at the way your child sees you. It will take some time before each of you really become comfortable and acclimated to this process, as a matter of fact, it will probably take several report cards before you are both completely honest with each other. But make a commitment to honesty and most of all make a commitment to getting "straight A's."

This exercise may seem corny but if you put forth a little effort it can definitely create open communication between you and your teenager. As males we have to be willing to do whatever it takes to develop close relationships with our children. This exercise is definitely a great start. Make a commitment to honesty and trust within your relationship with your child, and remember it's a process that goes on forever. I'm sure most of you reading have never tried anything like this but trust me it works. You simply have to decide you want to create great communication with your child, that's all.

So that is a brief overview of the four stages of your child's development. Let's go over them again:
1. Newborn Stage
2. Infant Stage
3. Adolescent Stage
4. Teenager

As fathers, we must commit to developing the necessary skills to assist our youth in developing their psychological and emotional skills so that they will be equipped to handle all the external pressure they are put under.

So, now that we have a better understanding of the developmental stages of our child's growth, let's take a look at some things we can do to assure our children will have the skills necessary to become confident, secure human beings.

SEXUALITY

This is definitely a very sensitive issue. Everyone has their own opinions, so I would like to share mine. I think it's important to first and foremost develop your own boundaries on this issue. Each person needs to take some time and decide what's appropriate to them based on their own values. I believe that we as parents have to educate ourselves first, and then we can discuss this issue openly with our children. We can no longer afford to let our children get their information from the streets. We must be able to discuss openly healthy sexuality. We must talk to our children about taking care of their own bodies. I believe it's important to be specific in our discussions about our sexual organs, and we shouldn't use euphemisms to teach our kids about their body parts. We should be comfortable using the correct anatomical names, penis and vagina, when talking to our children. Most importantly, we need to understand that sex education is needed, but it only teaches kids about the act of sex. On the other hand, sexuality deals with the reason behind the act. If we commit ourselves to developing self-esteem in our children, a lot of them will not have to act out sexually to feel loved. That is the key. *Teaching our children how to love themselves for who they are so they don't have to look outside of themselves for acceptance.* Our kids are faced with incredible obstacles, like AIDS and lots of other sexually transmitted diseases. We must do everything in our power to assist them in dealing with all this pressure. The key is nurturing and support from within the family structure. That also means educating ourselves, so that we can deal with these very important issues. In case you aren't comfortable talking to your kids openly about sex (most of us aren't), I would like to recommend that you get a copy of a video titled *"What kids want to know about sex and growing up"* by the Children's television workshop. Arsenio Hall and Magic Johnson also did a wonderful video called *"Time Out"* that will help you in discussing these very sensitive issues with your children. Please! We must make this top priority. Our kids lives are depending on us. Take action now!

DISCIPLINE

We never have to hit our children. If we commit ourselves to understanding child behavior, we will learn that corporal punishment does more harm than good. It is my belief that there is no such thing as a bad child. A child simply learns his behavior from the environment he's in. If we put more focus on providing nurturing supportive environments, then we will create nurtured, secure kids.

Without question, we usually parent the way we were parented. Take a moment and think about your own upbringing. If you remember receiving beatings, then you will probably rationalize and justify beating your own kids as normal parental behavior. I would like to suggest, that the "Old School" teaching of raising our kids is no longer acceptable. We have to recognize that there has been incredible progress in the understanding of childhood development. We must commit ourselves to learning these new methods. I often hear blacks say that using "Time-Out" as an alternate form of discipline is what white people do, but I assure you that we have several leading black psychologists that are now advocating not spanking our children. We need to understand that to discipline means to train not to hit. I think the old Bible passage: "Train up a child in the way they should go, and they will not stray away" means to guide and lead by example, not to beat your children. "Spare the rod and spoil the child" is another one of the old school teachings that in my opinion is definitely obsolete. We have to know that corporal punishment really doesn't work over the long run. It may get the child to be quiet for a short term, but the internal scars will remain long term.

Please give this some careful consideration. It is the key to developing our children's sense of well being.

In addition to physical punishment, we must also understand that verbal abuse can be just as damaging as physical abuse. When we scream at our children and use words like "stupid, retarded, ignorant, dummy," we only create those negative feelings within our children. Ultimately they internalize these words and it destroys their sense of self-worth. We must understand that words can hit harder than a fist and the emotional scars can last forever. All this negative input convinces the child that they aren't worthy and aren't important, and they usually act out in negative ways. We must do everything in our power to instill confidence and feelings of worthiness into our children. That means reassuring them that they are important and we care about them.

Because of the societal conditioning of our culture, as men, we have always been raised to be tough and prepared to survive. I realize the world seems like an unsafe place, and sometimes we think teaching our sons to be tough is the only way they can survive, but let me assure you that the best thing you can do for your son is provide love, nurturing and guidance and I promise he will be okay. I'm not saying there won't be confrontations, but do realize that if you develop a secure sense of confidence in your child and he knows that you care about him and will be there for him, the battle is already won. We cannot use words like "punk, sissy, faggot, crybaby or chump" and expect our kids to grow up confident and secure. These words only reinforce the stereotypical illusion that males are supposed to be tough, and the only thing it does is create feelings of inadequacy with in our kids. We must understand that punching on our children and trying to make them men by being tough only makes them afraid and angry. Ultimately it destroys their ability to create loving, open communication in all their relationships.

If you have been using these words (or any other negative type methods to raise your children), I beg you to reconsider and use more positive methods of discipline.

It is my belief that 90% of all our social ills come from how we raise our children. I believe that if we put forth a more concerted effort to raising our children properly, then we will no longer have to deal with problems like teenage pregnancy, drug abuse and high school dropouts. This has to be top priority in our lives. Take some time and get to know your kids, because they truly are a wonderful gift.

I want to close with an analogy for you to consider, please take some time and give it some careful consideration, ponder on it for awhile until your entire being has grasped the lesson in it.

If you go to a train station and look at the trains what do you see? Did you know that only the engine is considered the train? Everything behind the engine is considered a car. So the train's responsibility is to be the leader of all the cars that are following it. Without the train the cars couldn't move. No matter where the train goes the cars have to follow. If the train goes fast, then so do the cars, if the train goes slow the cars follow suit. It is the train's job to decide what course to take, and which direction it will lead its cars. The cars job is simply to follow the leader.

As men, we are the train in our children's lives. It is up to us to decide where we are going to lead our children. Without us, our cars just sit there waiting for us to make the first move. We have to be leaders because all our cars can do is follow us. If we go in the wrong direction our cars will follow us, whatever pace we set our cars will keep up with us. This is what it means to be a real man. To be the train and lead. To lead our cars in the right direction at just the right speed, not too fast or not too slow. If we go in the wrong direction whose fault is it? Definitely not the cars, because they are only following us. It's our fault and the time has come that we face up to this. We have to lead by example, we cannot adhere to the old philosophy of "Do as I say not as I do." It simply doesn't work.

Ask yourself a few questions:
If you are currently abusing your children,
    which direction do you think they will go?
If you're addicted to drugs or alcohol,
    where are you leading your children?
If you harbor hatred and anger towards another race,
    what lessons are you teaching your children?
If you don't love and respect yourself,
    how can they be expected to?

We have to make this top priority in our lives. As we enter the next millennium it is imperative that our children are prepared to continue to keep this the greatest country in the world. Our future and the future of our world depends on it. Remember, children learn from example, so please take the time to be the leader you are supposed to be!

YOUR CHILDREN ARE DIVINE GIFTS FROM GOD.

YOU MUST TREAT THEM AS SUCH.

Love Your Body!

It's The Only One You've Got!

HEALTH AND FITNESS

Who is the world's fastest man?
   Carl Lewis, *a black man*

Who is the only man to win eight consecutive Mr. Olympia, body building contests?
   Lee Haney, *a black man*

Who's the only man to ever score one hundred points in a single basketball game?
   Wilt Chamberlain, *a black man.*

Who's the only man to have played a professional football game and a professional baseball game on the same day?
   Dion Sanders, *a black man.*

Who dominates the four major sports of the U.S.
   Black Men.

Who leads the nation in most health related illnesses and death?
Including high blood pressure, diabetes, cancer and heart disease.
   Black Men

What's wrong with this picture?

   This is a paradox that I find very disturbing. As black men, we are the epitome of not only physical strength, but the perfection of the human body. There is no denying the incredible physical attributes of black men.
   With the incredible exposure we receive in this area, you would think that health and fitness would be something that black men hold sacred. But according to most statistics this isn't the case.
   Brothers, are you listening? We lead the nation in death!
   I'm sure the rationalization will be that so many of us live in poverty, and a lot of blacks are predisposed to certain illnesses. Obviously there is some validity to that, but my question is "Whose responsible for the food that 'you' put in your mouth?" Is it the governments responsibility to put you on an exercise program? I realize that there are a lot of us that may not have health care insurance. But no one is responsible for your health, except you. In order to avoid responsibility, we generalize and put the focus on blacks as a whole, but the truth is "You" are the one who picks up the food and puts it in your own mouth. So ask yourself "what am I feeding myself?"

   As a whole, most men don't take very good care of themselves physically. If you look at mortality rates for men verses women, you'll find that women normally outlast men in longevity by approximately 10 years. Why is that? Men obviously are better equipped physically to be stronger than women, and there are definitely more sports geared around men, so why is it that women outlive us? Are they somehow genetically superior?

I believe the answer is very simple. Women simply take better care of themselves because they don't let their ego get in the way of taking care of their bodies. As men, we come up with every excuse in the book to not take care of ourselves. We convince ourselves that real men (whoever they are) should eat whatever and whenever they want. So we justify our behavior by using that male ego. We sit down and stuff ourselves until we're about to pop, suck down a few beers and fall asleep in front of the television. We sometimes never consider the consequences of our gluttony. So what are the consequences? Heart disease, diabetes, cancer and death!

Of course we deserve this luxury because we work so hard. Fear plays a large part in keeping us from really taking care of ourselves. We may have a small problem that we blow up into a large problem simply because we're scared of what the doctor "might" say. Then we become immobilized and won't take any action because things "might" be bad. Speaking for myself, this practice is pretty "Stupid".

We have to make a commitment to take care of our bodies and not be afraid to see a doctor if necessary. This process starts with prevention. It truly amazes me to see brothers take their cars to be serviced on a regular basis, yet they don't have a preventative maintenance program for their bodies. They think nothing of spending hundreds of dollars to fix up their cars yet won't invest a couple of hundred dollars to get an annual physical.

So what excuses are you using to not take care of yourself physically?

1. No Time?
2. Health Clubs too expensive.
3. You really don't need to exercise?
4. Uncle Fred smoked three packs a day and still lived to be 100.
5. You don't want to walk around looking like a jock?
6. Too old?
7. Past injuries?
8. That's what white people do?

The list could go on forever. Of course you realize these are all just rationalizations you've created to keep you from being healthy. I really don't need any scientific evidence to prove to you the benefits of exercise, or do I? I'm sure everyone knows the benefit of exercise, most people simply refuse to give themselves the benefit of not only looking great, but feeling great too.

My job isn't to convince you of the benefits, but to provide you with some information that may assist you in starting and maintaining some type of workout program. As I've mentioned, I am not an expert, but as a former fitness trainer I'm sure I can guide you in the right direction.

Have you noticed that no matter what program an expert might suggest, there's always another expert that has an entirely different opinion. We have so many so called experts most people don't know who to listen to. So the secret is to get to know your own body. With a little research and a commitment to fitness, you can learn to listen to your body like no one else can. Once you do that you can make your own decisions as to what's best for your own body.

I would like to share some basic concepts and philosophies that have worked for me. Each human body is a unique individual expression. But knowing some basic fundamental elements will help you on your way.

CHECK-UPS

This is the best place to start. Although you may not need a complete physical, it's a good idea to see what shape you're in. Here is a list of some things to check first.

1. Blood pressure
2. Cholesterol level
3. Weight (Check for proportion to height and age)
4. Body Fat %
5. Resting Heart Rate

Most of this can be done pretty inexpensively. There are clinics and health fairs that provide these services at little or no cost. Always consult your physician before you take on any major change in physical activity.

DIET & DIETS

I am definitely not a dietician. I will suggest that you start paying closer attention to what you eat. As black males we have to recognize that all that fried soul food is killing us. We need to be aware of the importance of a healthy well balanced diet. Go to a bookstore and get you a book on nutrition and diets. Learn a little bit about calories, carbohydrates and protein. When it comes to losing weight, most diets don't work when they're used without exercise. The biggest advantage, and most significant reason to exercise versus just dieting is strengthening your heart. When you diet you may lose weight but you do nothing for your heart.

I also need to stress the psychological factor involved with dieting. In a large number of cases it's not what you're eating but what's eating you. You need to take an honest look at your emotional state whenever you have a weight problem. It could be that the weight is the symptom of a much larger problem. Love yourself enough to take action to get to the root of your problems. Otherwise you will create a cycle of never-ending pain and abuse. I would also like to add that the key to healthy eating is moderation. Instead of always eating to get stuffed, simply cut back on the amount of food you're eating. A little trick I use is to always drink plenty of fluids. I normally get extra glasses of whatever beverage I'm having and after eating in small proportions I simply fill up on the drink. It gives you the feeling of being full without the extra calories.

AEROBIC & ANAEROBIC EXERCISE

Without getting really technical, these are your two basic areas of exercise. Aerobic means with air or oxygen, and anaerobic means without air or oxygen. I describe anaerobic as with weights and aerobic as without weights. I'm sure you have heard the term "Cardiovascular exercise." That is basically the same as aerobic exercise. What you are doing is getting your heart rate to increase significantly so that your body has to take in more air and oxygen. (Heavy breathing.) Have you ever wondered why the aerobic instructors are always moving and throwing their hands up over their heads? It works like this: as your body keeps moving, your heart has to pump blood to those muscles that are doing the extra work. The more you swing your arms and jump up and down, the more blood you need. As you maintain an exercise routine, your heart strengthens and as time progresses the heart gets stronger and is able to pump the same amount of blood with fewer beats.

When you first begin a routine, let's imagine that your heart beats at seventy-five beats per minute. As your heart strengthens, that number is reduced. After a few weeks it now only takes your heart sixty-five beats to pump the same amount of blood. When a person has high blood pressure the heart is beating more times than necessary to pump the blood throughout the body. Let's just say it beats 100 beats per minute. As you start exercising, you strengthen the heart and it takes a lot of stress off your heart and arteries. Remember, the stronger the heart, the fewer beats it takes to pump the blood. That's the reason exercise is so important. It is the only way to actually strengthen the heart. Another great benefit of exercise is the removal of cholesterol. Cholesterol is the fatty substance that blocks the arteries and doesn't let blood flow properly. As you exercise, you create what's called the good cholesterol that reduces the amount of fatty deposits within the arteries. It's like using drano; it cleans out your pipes.

Without question, this is the most important form of exercise. Whenever you go walking, that's aerobic exercise. Jogging, cycling and swimming are also forms of aerobic exercise.

The key to any form of exercise is consistency. You must maintain your routine on a consistent basis in order to reap the full benefits. When doing aerobic exercise an ideal program would be a minimum of three days a week and each routine would be at least thirty minutes in length.

Whenever you start a routine and then stop, it's just like starting over again. A good rule of thumb is to think of your muscles as having memory. If you don't remind them on a consistent basis, they forget what you've taught them. After you skip a few days, they have to be retrained all over again.

Although this is the most important type of exercise, most men don't participate. As I've mentioned, our ego gets in the way and we're more concerned about how we look on the outside, than what's really going on inside. We usually head straight for the weights (anaerobic) and work on pumping up our pecks and creating bulging biceps. Just because you see a person with a great body, that does not necessarily means he's in good shape. It's easy to pump up the chest, but if you aren't strengthening your heart you're skipping the most important element of exercise. Aerobic exercise is the most important. Please make sure you make it a part of your routine.

Start off with an aerobic program and work your way up. The reason most people don't stick to their routines is they try to do too much at once. Don't start off by depriving yourself of your favorite foods. Once you began working out on a consistent basis and start seeing some results, you will automatically become more aware of what you're eating. Remember, consistency is the key. I suggest that you simply start by doing some form of aerobic exercise every other day for at least thirty minutes at a time. Once you become comfortable with that routine and have established consistency (eight weeks or so), then move to the next phase.

Then you can start adjusting your diet and getting more serious with your program. Most people last an average of two to three months then quit. If you can commit yourself to get past the three months, you're home free.

Body Fat

What is fat? Fat is nothing more than stored food or fuel. If you're over-weight, then it's your body's way of saying you're taking in more fuel than you're burning off. The old myth used to be that as you got older you automatically gained weight. The truth is it isn't your age that's the problem, it's a sedentary lifestyle that causes the excess baggage. If you continue to stay active you will continue to eliminate the excess fuel.

So let's talk about burning fuel.

The first thing we normally do when we want to lose weight, especially if it's a beer belly, is to do sit-ups. This myth has been perpetuated for many years. The truth is sit-ups have absolutely nothing to do with removing that pot belly. If you will tighten up your stomach as if someone were about to hit you, you will notice that the muscle is underneath the fat. As you do sit-ups you only strengthen the abdominal muscles. The key to losing weight is to "*burn off*" the excess fuel metabolically.

Think of it this way:

As you're exercising, the heart begins to work harder to pump blood throughout the body. As your heart beats harder, it sends a message to your brain that it needs more fuel. The brain receives the message, then contacts the fat cells which in turn starts burning the stored fat. The longer you keep your heart rate up, the more fat you burn. This is why aerobic exercise is so important. It helps burn the extra fuel that is stored throughout your body. It also strengthens your heart so that you can increase the length of your aerobic exercise.

Once you've established some consistency in your aerobic routine, then it's time to move to anaerobic exercise or working out with weights.

The purpose of working out with weights, is to tone and strengthen muscles. Once you've lost those extra pounds and strengthened that ticker of yours, then you want to make sure you stay nice and firm. Have you ever heard the term "Hardbody?" A hardbody is a person that keeps their body fat to a minimum, thereby his body is mostly muscle. What you feel is the muscle in the body versus the fat. Let's go into detail a little bit.

Let's imagine that you weigh 200 pounds. You take a body fat percentage test and it says that your percentage is 20 percent. What that means is that 40 of your 200 pounds is fat. Your lean body weight is 160 pounds and your fat weight is 40 pounds Total body weight 200 pounds.

If you weigh 200 pounds and your fat percentage is 10 percent, then you have 20 pounds of fat and a lean body weight of 180 pounds.

If you had two individuals that fit these categories, which do you think would look the heaviest?

The person with the highest body fat percent will always look heavier. The reason is that muscle is heavier than fat, yet fat simply takes up more room. The leaner you are from a body fat perspective the slimmer you will appear. This can cause a lot of confusion for people that are just starting a workout program. They maintain a routine then they realize that their gaining weight, what's happening is their converting fat to muscle and muscles are heavier. So the best thing to do is go by your measurements not your weight. Sometimes you will lose inches before you lose weight. Don't be alarmed it's normal. The greatest benefit of maintaining a low body fat percentage is your metabolism. Your metabolism is the process in which your body converts fat to fuel, or the speed in which you burn calories. The higher your metabolism the faster your body burns calories. The lower your body fat percentage the higher your metabolism. So by maintaining a low body fat percentage the food you eat is used up quicker. Therefore it's easier to maintain your weight. So concentrate on maintaining a moderate body fat percentage. It will assist you in keeping your weight under control.

WEIGHT TRAINING.

So you decide you want to workout with weights. There are basically two types, free weights and universal weights (or machines). The main difference is that machines work large groups of muscles and free weights can concentrate on isolating individual muscles. Most people don't need free weights. Unless you decide to really get serious about weight lifting, you can get just as much out of machines versus free weights. The other advantage of machines versus free weights is the machine is safer and easier to use. You won't necessarily need anyone to spot you, so you don't have to worry about dropping the weights on yourself.

What you want to do is design a program that works all major muscle groups. There are hundreds of programs out there; and I like several different ones personally, but it's going to

Health and Fitness

be up to you to make a decision of what's best for you. I will share a program that I found extremely successful. It combines both aerobic and anaerobic exercise. It uses universal equipment and can be easily adapted to most body types.

First I'll give you the list of exercises:
1. Leg Press: Works the quadriceps (the huge muscles in front of your legs)
2. Leg Curls: Works the hamstrings or the muscles in back of the legs
3. Bench Press: Works the outer chest area
4. Seated Fly: Works the inner chest area
5. Lat Pulldown: Works back
6. Tricep Pressdown: Works muscles in back of your arms
7. Bicep Curl: Works muscles in front of your arms
8. Crunches: Tightens the stomach muscles (replaces sit-ups)

These eight exercises will basically cover all major muscle groups. Invest in a fitness magazine to get the full understanding of how the exercises work and how the major muscle groups work.

Let's assume you decide to join a health club or purchase a universal set for your home.

The first thing you need to do is warm up. Start on an exercise bike or do some stretching exercises. This is extremely important because it will decrease your chance of injury. Do a little homework and create a stretching routine for yourself.

After you've warmed up, start at the top of the list with the leg press exercise. If you're not working with a trainer, you will need to figure out how much weight to use. A rule of thumb is to start with a weight that you can lift at least fifteen times (reps) without any pain. Once you establish that weight, make a note of it so you can refer to it on a regular basis and also use it as a way to measure your progress. Establish your workout weight on each machine using the fifteen rep criteria. Once you have established your weights on all the machines, then note them on a chart of some sort. Start at the leg press and do fifteen reps. Upon completion, ride a stationary bike or do jumping jacks for one minute, then go to the next exercise. Repeat the process until you have completed all exercises except the crunches. Don't push yourself too hard. The way this program works is by combining erobic and anaerobic exercise. As you're losing the weight, you are also tightening the skin and strengthening the muscles. Remember consistency is the key. This program will provide you with a complete body workout. If you stick to it for two weeks, I promise you will experience incredible results.

Once you start noticing results, and the exercises become too easy simply increase the weight. You can also increase the number of sets. Which means you would lift the weight fifteen times, take a two minute break, then lift it fifteen more times before you ride the bike.

The old saying "No pain, no gain" is obsolete. You will experience some stiffness, but that's only because of inactivity. Creating pain is one of those male ego beliefs. You shouldn't experience that because we're only working to tone the muscle not necessarily make it grow. Pain comes from tearing the muscle to get it to increase in size; that's another book. What we're concerned with is designing a healthy routine that you will stick to and give you great results.

To complete the routine we will finish with crunches, which is the correct way to do sit ups. There are two things to remember. First, your head should not come up off the floor more than approximately 30-40 degrees. When you do the old type sit-ups, you not only waste a lot of motion and energy, but you run the risk of actually injuring your back. The secret is to focus on the muscle as you do the exercise. Feel the muscle tighten, then release. Because the abdominal muscles are a bunch of little stringy muscles joined together, you can always do as many as your little heart desires without fear of overworking them. They can be the most difficult muscles to respond sometime, but stick to it. I suggest that you do them until you drop at the end of your routine. The second thing to remember is, don't grab the back of your neck! This puts an incredible strain on your back spinal cord! Avoid it at all cost. Simply rest your hands on your stomach and complete the exercise.

After you've worked through your program, go through your stretching routine again. You will notice that stretching will be a little easier because the muscles are warmed up and full of blood. Use the stretch period as a cool down period.

Do this routine every other day. If you get overenthusiastic and want to exercise everyday, remember to not lift weights two consecutive days. Allow your muscles one day of rest. You can however do any type of aerobic exercise on a daily basis. Crunches can also be done everyday.

This is just an example of a routine. It's up to you to do some homework and use these suggestions as guidelines.

FLEXIBILITY

This is another area that most people neglect (myself included). But working on our flexibility should also be included in our routine. Stretching is important because it loosens and helps elongate the muscles. Remember when you were a kid and you could put your foot in your mouth? The truth is, if you really committed yourself, you could still do it. What happens is the muscles contract and get tight when we don't use them. By stretching on a regular basis you will notice your flexibility return and feel a lot better in the process. Can you still touch your toes? You may want to try a yoga class.

RELAXATION & MEDITATION

Of all the things I've learned over the years, this is probably the most important. Four years ago, to relax meant to sit in front of the television with a wine cooler and watch football games. I usually worked 50 - 60 hour weeks and had no idea what total relaxation meant. There were some psychological reasons for my inability to relax, but once I recognized them I learned to really just let go and unwind. For me personally I really didn't understand what stress was a few years ago. But now I'm always aware of the signals my body and mind send me when I need to just chill for awhile and relax.

Most people in western cultures look at meditation as strange. I personally make it one of the highest priorities in my life. There is no right or wrong way to meditate. I won't go into detail, but I highly recommend you give it a try. Start off with a meditation tape; Louise Hay has some good ones. You will notice that your mind will have a field day with telling you how corny this is. Just disregard that voice and do it anyway; you will slowly work into a routine. As with any exercise, you will have to train your mind to be still. With a little effort and consistency you will notice incredible results. Ask yourself when was the last time you were completely relaxed? We live in such a fast paced, stress-filled society, we forget how to just be still for a while. The results of this are ulcers, stress, alcoholism and heart attacks, to name a few. Invest some time just for yourself and incorporate a little time each day to get away from the stress. I promise, you will be a lot more productive. "Try it, you'll like it."

MASSAGE & CHIROPRACTIC

If you've never had a full body massage you are missing one of life's greatest pleasures. There are lots of benefits, but relaxation and improved circulation are probably the most important. You've got to do this at least once. If you do, you will be hooked for life. Initially I was very skeptical about chiropractic techniques. I hadn't planned on trying it until I experienced a back injury. After a few visits, I was sold. I try to stay away from doctors as much as possible, but once you experience results the way I did, they really aren't that bad. Like any other doctor, you should always check references and even get second opinions. Chiropractic gets two thumbs up from me.

DRUGS & ALCOHOL

I'm not going to preach, but I will plead that if you are currently abusing drugs or alcohol, please get help. I'm sure you realize the harmful effects these things have on your body. The question now is, what are you going to do about it? You need to realize that alcohol and drug abuse really isn't your fault, but it is definitely your problem. You need to understand that the effects of these things not only affect you but the people close to you. If you won't do it for yourself, please do it for the people who care about you (myself included). If you smoke, make a commitment to quit. Do it at your own pace; simply get it done. Take action. Now! You deserve to be healthy. Success in the 90's means taking care of our bodies and making sure they're operating effectively and efficiently. Without our health, how are we going to enjoy all our other successes?

To summarize this chapter, I'd like to say that it is imperative that we, as Black males, make a commitment to health and fitness. We lose too many lives to problems that are easily prevented. Another area is murder. We have got to stop killing each other (or anyone for that matter). If we reduce the incidence of drunkenness and drug intoxication, we will see a dramatic decrease in deaths. This needs to be top priority. We have to take responsibility for all our brothers who are dying needlessly on our streets in our neighborhoods. The time for action is now! It starts one human being at a time. Take some time to ask yourself how you can be part of the solution instead of part of the problem.

In addition, we must take responsibility for our sexual behavior. We must understand that AIDS is not just a homosexual disease. It is a disease that knows no sexual preference or color. It does not discriminate against age or gender. It is a deadly menace to our world and it must be stopped. Please take whatever precautions are necessary to protect yourself and those you come in contact with. This is serious! We have to do what ever it takes to stop the spread of this awful disease.

I know we can overcome these problems; we've survived much worse, but it's going to take a united effort. All you have to do is care enough.

Health and Fitness

Just Do It!

Just Do It!

Just Do It!

Just Do It!

Just Do It!

Success is to be measured not so much by the position that one has reached in life, as by the obstacles which he has overcome while trying to succeed!

Booker T. Washington.

SUCCESS AND WEALTH

I read an article in *Ebony* magazine asking the question, "What would Dr. Martin Luther King Jr. say about the status of Black Americans today?" As I sat there and pondered this question, I asked, "What would I say to Dr. King if I had the opportunity to speak to him?" So I pretended that I had one week to take Dr. King around the country.

If I had that opportunity, I think the first thing I would do is take him to my favorite bookstore. While there, I would share with him some of my favorite readings. I think he would be impressed to see the wide selection of magazines put out by black editors and publishers. I would point out magazines like *Essence, Ebony, Upscale, Ebony Man, Black Enterprise, Interrace, Emerge* and *Black Elegance* to name a few. I would then make sure that he purchased a copy of *Think and Grow Rich, a Black Choice* by Dennis Kimbro, *37 Things Every Black Man Should Know* by Errol Smith and of course I would provide him with an autographed copy of *Brothers, Are You Listening?* by yours truly. I'm sure he would be delighted to see that we've opened a lot of doors in success, motivational and inspirational readings. Of course I wouldn't leave out authors like Terry McMillian, Marion Wright Edelman or Maya Angelou either.

After our trip to the bookstore, we could relax and stop by the video store and rent a few movies. Although I realize Dr. King never advocated violence, I think he would have enjoyed *Passenger 57* with Wesley Snipes. I think he would have experienced an incredible amount of excitement seeing a black man in the leading role of an action adventure movie. We would also rent *Boomerang* with Eddie Murphy and I know he would have swelled with pride to see a film with so many intelligent beautiful black men and women. I've heard Dr. King had a great sense of humor, so I'm sure he would have laughed until he cried while we watched Whoopi Goldberg in *Sister Act*. I'm sure he would have wanted to congratulate John Singleton on being the youngest director ever nominated for an academy award for his film *Boys In The Hood*. I think he would agree with me that it is definitely one of the finest films ever created.

Of course I could take him to see some of the Blockbuster films that are currently playing on the big screen like *Above the Rim, The Inkwell*, and *Crooklyn* but since I only have a week we'd better get around to some other successes.

Of course we can turn on the television and see some incredible success stories. Although I watch very little television I would show him shows like *Living Single, Sinbad, In Living Color, Martin,* and one show I really enjoy, *Family Matters*. I know beyond a shadow of a doubt that he would get some great laughs out of watching the hilariously funny Steve Erkle. Of course I would have to arrange an interview with the queen of the daytime talk shows Oprah Winfrey. We would also have to make a guest appearance with Montel Williams. Of course we can't leave out the king of entertainment, Mr. Bill Cosby. I think I would persuade Dr. King to try to get Mr. Cosby to do another sitcom like *The Cosby Show*. I really miss it.

All in all, I think he would be pleased with the presence of so many Blacks on the big screen and television. I think he would agree that "we're not where we want to be, but thank God we're not where we used to be."

Of course I would have to take him to see the Houston Rockets basketball team. I'm sure he would be in awe of the incredible talents of Hakeem Olajuwon, who in my opinion is the premier center in the league. Dr. King would undoubtedly salute all the incredible accomplishments of black athletes and their contributions to sports. I'm sure he would like to acknowledge Mr. Shell for becoming the first black head coach in the N.F.L. and also Mr. Green (the second black head coach) for following in his footsteps. There would be no doubts in his mind that we have made incredible strides in this particular area.

Another person I would introduce him to would be Mae Jemison, the first black female astronaut. Not only is she extremely intelligent, but she's also gorgeous. (Actually I'm the one that wants to meet her.) I'm not sure what Dr. King's taste in music was, but I'm sure he would have enjoyed listening to Awadagin Pratt, the first black classical pianist to win a national classical event. I'm also sure he would have been pleased to know that for one week in 1993, the top 10 songs on billboard were all sung by black artists; it was definitely a first in the music business.

I can only imagine how proud he would have been to have watched Jesse Jackson make a serious run for the presidency of the United States. A part of me says that would have been his proudest moment. Watching Rev. Jackson pull people of all races colors and creeds together for the common good of this great country surely would have brought tears to his eyes. Seeing that would have let him know that he didn't die in vain and his dream is definitely still alive. I would take him to meet Gov. Wilder, Mayor Dinkins, Senator Brauhn and Clarence Thomas. I think he would be happy to see blacks choosing their political candidates based on their own individual views rather than just conforming to the norm. I'm sure he would have been delighted to meet President Clinton. I personally would thank him for making an honest attempt to bring the country together. I was really moved by the number of black talent he had perform at his inauguration. I'm also glad to see that he's trying his best to give blacks and other minorities an opportunity to participate in the political structure. Maybe Dr. King's word of advice to the president would be: "Run your administration with love and divine guidance, and you will make this the greatest country in the world."

We would make a trip to N.Y., and visit the N.Y. Stock Exchange and watch them trade stock from B.E.T. We would contact some of the large Black-owned corporations like Cross Colors or Beatrice Foods, congratulate them on their success and encourage them to motivate others to start their own businesses. I think he would be amazed at the number of black businesses that are truly successful.

As we wound down our week together, I would definitely invite him to one of my own motivational seminars. I know I would be able to not only motivate him, but also inspire him the way he inspired me. I'd also invite the great motivational speaker Les Brown. Together I'm sure we would bring the house down. Dr. King would surely recommend that Mr. Brown and I continue our positive message of self empowerment. I'm sure he would agree with our position of self responsibility and personal improvement. I'd make sure that he received some videotaped footage of this empowering event.

Finally, I would use the last hours with him, to ask for guidance and strength to empower me to follow in his footsteps. I would take this opportunity to thank him for his courage and his vision. I would ask him what steps I needed to take in order to live my dreams and make a difference in the world. I obviously can't speak for Dr. King, but I believe he would tell me, first and foremost, that I need to know God is with me. I have to make that first priority. Understanding that there is a power greater than myself at work, will give me the strength to overcome any obstacle. Once I have developed my faith, I have to be able to believe in myself. I have to know that God has provided me with certain gifts and talents to be used in His service. I have to be committed to developing these gifts and use them to be of maximum service to my Creator. Understanding that all the answers to my questions can be found within, and that it is my responsibility to go within to find the answers. Although I know God is always with me, I have to be willing to do it alone. Most people will tell you what you cannot do, but you can't listen to the negative doom sayers. If God has a plan for you, he will reveal it to you and you only. You will obviously need other people to assist you, but you have to recognize that it's your dream. The only thing you need is God, he'll do the rest.

Last, but definitely not least, you have to do it with love. This is probably the most important. Love is the most powerful force of the universe. It is literally God. It is the animating force of life, and it can move mountains. If you do everything with love you are expressing all that God is and the world will be at your beck and call. It is the lesson taught by all great spiritual leaders, and when you adhere to it you become a light for God to shine through. You can literally light up the world.

So I think his last words to me would be:

1. Believe in God
2. Believe in yourself
3. Do everything with love

I know it would be a tearful farewell. I would embrace him, draw upon his love and power, and thank him for his divine guidance and inspiration. As we said good-bye, I think I would hear one last phrase that would let me know that I was on the right path. I think Dr. King would reflect back over our week together, would look me in the eye and say: "Well done, my Brother, well done." And I would just smile with tears in my eyes and say, "Thank you, my Brother, for leading the way."

It truly amazes me that some people say that, as black people, we are no better off today than we were thirty years ago. I do not deny the problems, but I simply choose to focus on what's right. I remember not seeing black people on television at all so when I do see them I realize we're moving in the right direction. A lot of people say I'm too optimistic. but that's the reality I choose to create. My main philosophy is: "We're not where we want to be, but thank God we're not where we used to be." Whenever I see a black success story I immediately say "Way to go, my Brother (or Sister). "

Without question, we have experienced some incredible successes within the last thirty years and without question the sky is the limit from here on out. The question now becomes are you willing to be one of those success stories? As we position ourselves for the 21st century, I see an unlimited amount of possibilities for anyone that's willing to put forth the effort. As we shift to the new world economy those opportunities are even greater.

So ask yourself, "What do I see?"

Do you see a world that's falling apart? Do you see a world wide recession? Do you believe that there really aren't any opportunities out there? Is your life filled with fear? Are you concerned that you may not have a job tomorrow? If you answered yes to any of those questions, you have obviously created a belief that there is something outside of yourself that is responsible for your success. The truth is you and only you are responsible for your success. Not your job, not your color, not your spouse only you. Some of you may not believe that but let me clarify it for you.

First of all, I know that you have the power within you to create incredible wealth and success. Anyone reading this book can actually go out and start their own company if they wanted to. Of course everyone isn't going to do that so what else could they do.

If you are currently employed ask yourself these questions:

1. Do I give 100 percent to my job?
2. Am I taking every opportunity to make sure I have the knowledge that could assist me in moving up the corporate ladder?
3. Have I updated my job skills to create more opportunities for growth?
4. What is my attitude towards my employer?
5. Do I get along well with my coworkers?
6. Am I experiencing burnout and feel like my job is going nowhere?
7. Have I looked for other opportunities?
8. Would I hire myself if I were an employer?
9. Do I call in sick when that isn't the case?
10. Do I love or hate my job?

After you have asked yourself these questions, take a minute and ponder them for awhile. If you are currently afraid of the future I can guarantee that there is something within your control that you could do to remove that fear.

For example, If you are currently afraid of losing your job, ask yourself what kind of job you are doing. It's easy to place responsibility on something or someone outside of ourselves.

Success and Wealth

But as soon as we take responsibility we gain control of our own destiny. As an employer, I've had to deal with several employees that would not take responsibility for themselves and would therefore blame me for their failure.

I remember a case where I hired a young brother because his mother was a friend of mine. I assured him that he would not receive any preferential treatment, and he should expect to pull his own weight. At first he was filled with excitement and enthusiasm, he told me that he was happy to be working for a brother and he would make sure he didn't let me down. After a week he decided that since we were both black he could maintain an unprofessional attitude towards me. He started out by trying to use the "Come on brother-man approach." He would show up late and then expect me to "Cut him some slack." I informed him that his behavior would not be tolerated. His behavior became worse and his attitude continued to decline. Each time I disciplined him he tried to use the fact that we were both black and I shouldn't be so hard on him. After several written reprimands and countless verbal ones I had to terminate him. The day of his termination he came in late and tried to give me some sad excuse. I had actually given him more chances than I should have because of my friendship with his mom, but he accused me of being too hard on him. As he was leaving my office he told me how unfair I was and he said that if he had been white I probably wouldn't have fired him.

That is a story of someone who refuses to take responsibility for their success. Ask yourself if you know anyone like that.

When we decide to take control of our own destinies, we realize that there are always things we can do to assure our success. The first thing we have to do is evaluate where we are right now, then decide if we want to be somewhere else.

Lets start with where you are.

List ten things that you can do to improve your job performance.

1. _____
2. _____
3. _____
4. _____
5. _____
6. _____
7. _____
8. _____
9. _____
10. _____

Make a commitment to do at least five of them this week. Then do the other five the following week. Each week make a list in the area that needs improvement and commit to doing more than is expected of you. Remember CANI™, Constant And Never-ending Improvement. It's definitely applicable in this situation. You will be amazed at what happens when you take the initiative. Your boss will too. Remember you are the one responsible for your success. Here's a great saying that you should keep in your mind. "If it's to be, it's up to me." So wherever you are right now, and whatever you are doing make sure you are doing your best. When you put forth a little extra effort you get twice the benefits. First, you get the job done better. Secondly, there is an internal feeling of pride that comes from doing your very best. When you do things for your own satisfaction, you don't need anyone's approval but your own.

Now let's look at where you're going.

Write down ten goals you want to accomplish within your organization (i.e. raises, promotions sales goals)

1. _____
2. _____
3. _____
4. _____
5. _____
6. _____
7. _____
8. _____
9. _____
10. _____

Be realistic and put a quantifiable time frame next to each one of them. Commit yourself to a date of completion. Each time you accomplish a goal write "Victory" next to it, and date it. Once you complete ten, write ten more and start over. You have to condition yourself to stretch a little. Don't settle for mediocrity; always shoot for excellence. If you're in a dead end situation don't just sit there moping, take action. Start sending out resumes, take some networking courses, get some exposure for yourself. Talk to your friends about possible opportunities. If you are in a position that you hate, everybody loses, you and your employer. Set yourself up for a win-win situation. Even if you don't necessarily like your job, always do your best until you find something better. There is a lot of power in gratitude. If you learn to count your blessings, no matter what situation you're in, I promise you will create better situations.

The main thing to remember is:

No one is responsible for your success, except you! Think about It!

Now that you've grasped success, let's talk about wealth.

Random House Dictionary defines wealth as "1. A great quantity of money, or property, or value; 2. A plentiful amount; 3. All goods that have a monetary or exchange value; 4.

Valuable contents or produce."

I like John Roger's definition: " Wealth is health, happiness, abundance, prosperity, riches, loving, caring, sharing, learning, knowing what we want, opportunity, enjoying and balance."

I believe wealth is actually a way of looking at life.

Because of the society we live in, a large majority of us have bought into the belief that wealth is money. Of course money is a form of wealth, but I believe money is a very small part of wealth. During 1983-1987 my entire world revolved around the accumulation of money and material possessions. As a matter of fact my entire identity was wrapped up in material things. At the time I was earning $50K a year, I was living in a $80K home, and I had a wallet filled with every major credit card imaginable. By societies standards I was wealthy. But something was missing. I tried everything in my power to create an image of wealth on the outside, but I definitely didn't feel wealthy on the inside.

As I mentioned in the previous chapters, I went through a divorce, bankruptcy and foreclosure. But it wasn't until I lost everything that I was able to feel wealth on the inside. If you will notice the way I put together the chapters for this book, you might recognize that each chapter covers a specific aspect of my life. Each chapter takes you through a different learning experience. Each lesson that I learned about myself brought me closer to "True Wealth." When I put all the chapters together, I create wealth and balance. When I leave out a portion, I don't feel complete. My hope is that you will do the same. We have to realize that true peace and joy comes from *balance*, and we must commit ourselves to creating that balance.

Since I've covered several different aspects of wealth in the other chapters, this chapter will deal with monetary wealth. As usual, I don't claim to have all the answers, but I would like to share my experiences that have taught me a little about financial wealth.

Because of my love for business, I had figured out the basic ground rules for creating financial wealth at an early age:

1. Get a job that pays well.
2. Invest in a home or property
3. Have an investment that pays you something.

These are the three areas that I would like to focus on.

1. Getting the Job.

Getting a job that pays well is completely up to you. Only you can define what getting paid well equates to. For some it may be $20,000 per year, for others it might be $1,000,000. A lot of us get caught up in society's definition of financial independence, which usually includes millions of dollars. But in all sincerity, a person could be making $15,000 per year and be financially independent and happy. Take some time and think about this. Ask yourself these questions:

1. What is my earning potential?
2. What is the minimum annual salary I want to make?

3. What is the maximum I think I can make?
4. What skills do I have, and how can I convert them to money?
5. What do I enjoy doing?
6. What am I good at?
7. What am I willing to do to create the job I want?
8. Do I have what it takes to be my own boss?
9. Will my spouse support me in a possible career change?
10. What the hell am I waiting for? It's definitely time for a change!

Now I would like you to write down your dream job. Imagine if you could have any job in the world. Don't get analytical just start writing. Be specific.
What would it be like?
How much money would you be making?
What contributions could you make to society?
Will you be a manager? President? C.E.O.?
What kinds of "toys" could you reward yourself with?
What would be your ten year plan for success?
After you finish, make sure you didn't leave anything out. If you didn't start writing ask yourself why not?
Once you've decided what that job would be like, ask yourself what steps you need to take to make that dream a reality. Do you need to go back to school?
Do you have a great idea for a company that you've been thinking about?
What game plan do you need to put together to live your dream.
Spend a lot of time just thinking about your dream job and make notes of the thoughts and ideas that flow through your mind. Pretty soon the right idea will come (And you will know.) Then trust that still small voice and follow your heart.
Remember the power of belief! Whatever you wrote down, you can achieve, if you simply "Believe."

2. INVEST IN PROPERTY!

In order to create monetary wealth, we need to have some solid investments. Not everyone wants to own a home, but it is definitely a good idea to create some assets. Simply saving money is an asset. You should always learn to pay yourself first. Starting a savings account is probably the easiest way to start creating wealth. Ask yourself this question, If I had a three hundred dollar emergency, would I be able to handle it without borrowing it from someone else? I think the biggest problem people have with money isn't how much they make, but how much they spend. I used to make a sufficient amount of money, but I always seemed to be broke. Speaking from my own experience, the reason I was always broke was because I kept trying to create wealth from the outside. Because of the emptiness inside, the external things couldn't fill the void. It wasn't until I filled up the inside that the external wealth

Success and Wealth

became easier to accumulate. I highly recommend that you pick up a copy of *Wealth 101* by John Rogers and Peter McWilliams. They do a wonderful job of explaining this process. I guarantee that it will not only be informative, but also entertaining and funny.

So, the key is to control your spending. Have you ever done a budget? I've always hated personal budgets, as a matter of fact, I don't think I've ever balanced my checkbook in my life. But it wasn't until I actually wrote my expenditures down on paper that I finally realized that my outgo exceeded my income. This takes an incredible amount of discipline. But it is definitely worth the effort. You have to be very specific. You have to be willing to account for every penny that you spend before you can really create a solid budget. My recommendation is that, for one week, you write down every penny you spend. That means *every penny*. Keep a notepad in your car, at work and at home. Jot down everything for one week. I guarantee you will be surprised at how fast the little expenses add up to big expenses. Once you've figured out where the money is going, you can set your budget and get control of your spending. You can pick up a budget from your local Consumer Credit Counseling Service that can help you.

I personally don't believe that cars are good investments, unless, of course, it's a classic or antique. Because of the external mentality we have about wealth, a lot of people want to be seen in the "symbols of wealth." This gives a person that false sense of being wealthy. People drive around to be seen in these symbols, but soon find out that something's missing. I try never to generalize, but brothers are guilty of this in a number of cases. There is absolutely nothing wrong with owning a nice car. But when you're driving a car that you really can't afford because you want to appear wealthy, you are definitely setting yourself up for trouble. Maybe it would be a good idea to get a car that reduces your payments by a hundred dollars a month, then you could take that hundred dollars and put it in your savings account. Then you would really be accumulating wealth. It doesn't take a rocket scientist to figure out that something that depreciates in value as soon as you buy it, isn't a very good investment. The key is to create the job that you want, at the salary you need to have these things without overextending yourself. Don't try to fake it; you will only create unnecessary hardships in your life.

If you decide to take my advice and invest in your emotional and spiritual aspects of your life's wheel, you will really understand how we sell our souls to try to create wealth externally. My only objective is to get you to think about your current situation then decide to change. It's all up to you.

So, make the decision to invest in property that accumulates in value, and you will be on the right track.

3. INVEST IN SOMETHING THAT PAYS YOU BACK!

I am not a financial planner, but I will suggest that you speak to one. There are obviously hundreds of things to invest in; you simply have to make a decision to do so. Talk to someone about assisting you in putting together a plan for the future, not only yours, but your kids as well. Don't just think about today or tomorrow, think about ten years down the road. Where will you be financially? What do you plan on doing with all that money you've saved up. Think ahead, make plans. Here are a few things you need to be thinking about:

1. Creating investments that will generate income for you later.
   Example: I.R.A.s, Certificates of Deposits, Stocks, Mutual Funds
2. What Ifs? Security Valves.
   Example: Insurance, Trust funds
3. Cash generating investments
   Example: Rental Property, Business Partnerships

These are just a few of the areas to focus on if you are going to create success and wealth in the 90's. Take some time to learn a little about financial planning and it will pay big dividends in the end.

And remember, if an investment sounds too good to be true, it probably is a bad investment. Do some homework.

Don't forget:

Success and Wealth in the 90's is all up to you!!

Shoot for the Moon because, even if you miss, you will still be amongst the stars

I AM THERE!

Do you need Me?
I AM there.
You cannot see me yet I AM the light you see by.
You cannot hear Me yet I speak through your voice.
You cannot feel me yet I AM the power in your hands.
I AM at work though you do not understand my ways.
I AM at work though you do not recognize My works.
I AM not strange visions, I AM not mysteries.
Only in absolute stillness, beyond self can you know me as I AM
    and then but as a feeling and a faith.
Yet I AM there, Yet I hear. Yet I answer.
When you need me, I AM there
Even if you deny Me I AM there.
Even when you feel most alone, I AM there.
Even in your fears I AM there.
Even in your pain I AM there.
I Am there when you pray and when you do not pray.
I AM in you and you are in Me.
Only in your mind can you feel separate from me
    for only in your mind are the mists of yours and mine.
Yet only with you mind can you know me and experience me.
Empty your heart of empty fears.
When you get yourself out of the way I AM there.
You can of yourself do nothing, but I can do all.
And I AM in all.
Though you may not see the good, good is there for I Am there.
I AM there because I have to be, because I AM.
Only in me does the world have meaning, only out of me does the world take form.
Only because of me does the world go forward.
I AM the law on which the movement of the stars and
    the growth of living cells are founded.
I AM the love that is the laws fulfilling. I AM assurance.
I AM peace. I AM oneness. I Am the law that you can live by.
I AM the love that you can cling to. I AM your assurance.
I AM your peace. I AM one with you. I AM.
Though you fail to find me. I do not fail you.
Though your faith in me is unsure, My faith in you never wavers,
because I know you because I LOVE You, Beloved, I AM there.

                                         JAMES DILLET FREEMAN

GOD AND SPIRITUALITY

It is my belief that God is like "Coke™," He's "The Real Thing™!" Some people drink Coke™ out of a can, some drink it out of a bottle, some people drink it out of chilled glasses, and some people drink it out of plastic containers. Some people drink large amounts, and others drink small amounts. But ultimately, the container that it's in really doesn't matter. The only thing that matters is quenching your thirst with the Coke™.

God is the spiritual "Thirst Quencher!" Like Coke™, He can be held in different containers, but, ultimately, the container really doesn't matter. What does matter is if you are getting your spiritual thirst quenched. There are basically six containers that hold the "Real Thing™:" Christianity, Judaism, Hinduism, Confucianism, Islam, and Buddhism. Then you have the straws that are used to drink out of the container. Example: Christianity is the container and Methodist, Catholic, Protestant and Baptist are the straws. But as I've mentioned, they all contain God. Of course most religions think that their container is the right container, but that is simply their belief.

According to The New International Student Bible, 1st Corinthians, Chapter 12, Verse 12 states, "The body is a unit, though it is made up of many parts; and though it's parts are many, they form one body. So it is with Christ. For we were all baptized by one Spirit into one body—whether Jews or Greeks, slaves or free, and we were all given the one Spirit to drink."

It is my belief that that spirit is God. Unfortunately some of us wait until we reach such a point of spiritual dehydration, that we're close to death before we decide to drink of the Spirit.

This is what happened to me. Rather than try and push my beliefs on you, I would like to share with you my three year search to find "the right container." Without question, God is definitely not something I can even attempt to try and give you. It is something you have to want on your own. You have to be thirsty enough to want to quench your own thirst, and only you can decide which container you want to drink from. But maybe in following my journey it will lead you to the container that's right for you.

Immediately after my divorce I decided to go back to church. I was raised Baptist and always felt somewhat obligated to the Baptist straw which drew from the Christian container. I had reached that point of spiritual dehydration in my life so I was trying to find something that would not only quench my thirst, but also alleviate some of the pain. I became active for awhile, and attended on a regular basis for a few months. But something was missing, as I listened to the minister there were hundreds of questions that I had that were never sufficiently answered. Whenever I would ask specific questions, I was always told to pray about it. That was not the answer I was looking for. As I look back in retrospect, I realize I was only anesthetizing the pain by trying to force myself to believe something that deep down in my heart I didn't. It was easy for me to intellectualize the "Born Again Christian" experience but it never came from my heart. I had given some incredible testimonies about what Jesus had

* Coke™ and The Real Thing™ are trademarks of the Coca Cola Bottling Company done for me, but it all came from my head not my heart.

After five or six months I decided that I really needed to try something different. A part of me kept saying that there has to be more to this God experience than this, so I decided to try a different religion. I had a friend that had been trying for months to get me to try his church. He belonged to a Pentecostal Church and he assured me that I would really enjoy it because his church was always filled with the Holy Spirit. When I got there I definitely felt a Spirit but I'm not sure if it was Holy. (I do not intentionally want to offend anyone. If you belong to a Pentecostal church, please don't get upset with me sharing my experience. I support each and every one in their belief; I only ask that you do the same.)

This was my first experience in what I call "Holy Roller Churches." The minister had lots of energy, and he wasn't afraid to let the "Spirit move through him". He was jumping up and down and even rolling on the floor. Everyone appeared to be having a wonderful time. The volume was incredible. I could barely hear myself think.

Then all of a sudden, they all started speaking in tongues. I didn't know what to do. I just sat there and hoped they didn't expect me to do the same. My friend told me that if I would just surrender to God, he would speak through me. I informed my friend that I had a major issue with being in control, and as great as it sounded I refused to surrender to this process. Besides that, I was scared to death. I survived the service, but I knew it was definitely not for me.

After that experience, I decided that this was definitely the right thing for me to do. I concluded that each individual should have the right to choose their own church and it felt good to release the obligatory sense of having to be Baptist.

So I went church hopping.

I decided to try a Methodist church. When I first walked in, I liked the atmosphere. It was definitely the exact opposite of the Pentecostal church when it came to volume. As I listened to the service, I was impressed with the fact that the sermon actually made sense. The minister had constructed a talk with a solid introduction, an information filled body, and a logical conclusion. I really liked what was said. But there was too much conformity for me. Everyone seemed like little robots. It was as if they all had to say the right words and wear the right clothes to be accepted. So I decided to continue my search.

I was watching television one night and this minister was inviting everyone out to his "Oasis of Love." I thought to myself, "That sounds like a nice place. Let's give it a try." Even though the church was approximately an hour away, I committed myself to going. When I got there I was pleasantly surprised. The atmosphere was accepting and warm, and the people seemed friendly enough. It was a huge church, the type that you see showcased on television. There were TV monitors all over the place in case you were too far back to see the minister. The church grounds covered several acres and obviously had a very large membership. The thing that really caught my attention was the amount of interracial couples. I was really glad to see that. It made me realize that this was definitely an open-minded church.

The minister was a small fellow but he had a lot of charisma. He put his heart and soul

God and Spirituality

into his message and I even felt a little inspired. After the service he extended the invitation to join the church. Although I hadn't decided to join, I decided to stay after the service and get a little more information. I was taken to a room with a fellow that couldn't have been more than eighteen years old. He was obviously well informed about the church's belief and definitely held a strong conviction towards those beliefs.

He asked me why I had decided to attend their church. "Well, I was raised Baptist, yet I simply don't feel connected to God. As a matter of fact I have almost come to the conclusion that there really is no such thing."

He appeared a little shocked by that statement, but he automatically shifted to his religious duties. " Well, my brother, let me pray for you."

That wasn't what I wanted to hear, but I figured I would at least give him the courtesy to do his job. He put his hand on my forehead and started to pray. In all sincerity I hoped that something would happen. I had no idea what, but I was honestly trying to get something out of what he was saying.

All of a sudden he began speaking in tongues. I was startled, then he started to try to convince me that I could do the same. He assured me that God would speak through me if I would just surrender to his Holy Spirit. "Don't think about it," he said "just let God do the talking." Of course this poor fellow had know idea who he was talking to. Mister In-control, that's who. But I decided to make an honest attempt at allowing God to speak through me. But the more he kept praying, and speaking in tongues, the more ridiculous it became. After a few minutes I thought I had bit a hole in my lip from trying not to burst out laughing. The whole process seemed phony to me. I really wanted something to happen, but it definitely wasn't going to happen here.

I drove home a little disappointed and a little relieved at the same time. I had made an honest attempt to find God, but, I didn't, so I came to the conclusion that there really wasn't any such thing.

This was around the time when I had become involved with inner-child work. I then concluded that my brain held all the answers and through psychology and studying I could find all my answers. But there wasn't anything outside of this coconut sized mass of brain on my shoulders that had anything to do with anything.

As I became more and more connected emotionally, I gained enough evidence that all of man's mysteries could be solved by research and analysis.

Since the trauma I was exposed to as a child started my destructive behaviors, I could reverse that process through my recovery program. So my brain and mind really did have all the answers. I definitely didn't need this God entity in my life. I embraced my newfound knowledge, and decided that there really was no such thing as God.

I was participating in workshops and really growing emotionally. Relationships with people were intimate and real, and I literally had become a new person. But something still seemed to be missing. I decided I would call an atheist organization to see what their beliefs were. Since they didn't believe in God, I thought they may know something I didn't know. I contacted a group by phone, and they gave me their meeting dates and times. When I hung up the phone, something didn't feel right. There was something that said, "You don't belong there."

I sat there by the phone and wondered what I needed to do. As I sat there I thought about all the reasons I didn't believe in God. Then I came to the conclusion that the main reason I didn't believe in God was because Christianity, in my opinion, was the most irrational, illogical religion I had ever heard of. Then it hit me like a ton of bricks. Since I had tried only Christian religions, why not try something other than Christianity. Bingo!

I went to the library and started researching some eastern philosophy. As I read some of the Buddhist philosophies, something stirred in me for the first time. Their main focus seemed to be on Love. There wasn't all the damnation and guilt associated with Christianity, and a part of me came alive. They spoke of a state of "Nirvana," which is the ultimate oneness with the great Buddha. It sounded great to me. Now the question was how in the world am I going to get there. I started dabbling in a few other philosophies, Nation of Islam, and a little Hinduism. It felt great to finally be involved with something that didn't punish me for sins I hadn't even committed. I still hadn't found the one that really felt right, but, for the first time, I felt as if I were on the right path. I continued with my workshops and was continually becoming more and more healed. I had started to experience authentic happiness, and my life was definitely headed in the right direction.

Then I received my miracle.

I was participating in a personal effectiveness workshop, and one of the participants asked if I had ever heard of a church called "Unity." I told her I hadn't, and also informed her that I was pretty fed up with organized religion.

She told me that Unity was different. I asked if it were a Christian based religion and she said yes. "NO, thank you, I really don't want to be involved with Christians. I've had my share of Christian righteousness and judgmental-ness. I will pass on the Christianity thank you very much!"

"Before you become so closed minded, let me just share a couple of things with you. First of all, you know how you keep telling me how you love words like Empowerment, Transformation and Responsibility? Well, they use these words at Unity. Not only that, listen to what their slogan is: 'Teaching, Loving and inspiring people to be all they were created to be.' Isn't that great?"

"Sounds okay, but I don't know," I responded.

"Michael, I want you to listen to me. You are the most positive person I have ever met in my life. I realize that you will ultimately make your own choice, but I know this church is for you. Everything they do is positive. Sometimes they are so positive I don't even go, because I don't feel right. But you would fit right in, I just know it. Just give it a try. What have you got to lose?"

"I'll think about it."

After the workshop I went home and thought about it. I was pretty happy with my new found beliefs, and I was definitely not going to accept any duty and obligation from any

God and Spirituality

organization. But there was that part of me that started asking, "How does this Jesus character fit in the whole scheme of things?"

The next day I was flipping through the phone book, when the phone rang. I jumped from the table and knocked the phone book over in the process. After I finished my conversation, I picked up the phone book and threw it on the table. When it landed, it was open. When I sat down to look at it, there, at the top of the page, was an advertisement for Unity church.

I stared at it for a moment, then wrote the number down. I decided to give them a call and get their address. It turned out that they were just a few minutes away. That night I decided to just drive by and see what it was like. Although I knew no one would be there, I just wanted to get a feel for what the church was like. When I got there, I was surprised to see that they had this incredible bookstore. I could see through the window that they had a lot of my favorite authors. I got chills on my arms. I smiled and left, and waited for Sunday to get here so I could see what their teachings were.

After what seemed like an eternity, Sunday rolled around, and I was filled with excitement and enthusiasm. I couldn't wait to get there. I got there early to make sure I could get a good seat. When I arrived at the church, I sat outside for a little while just to see what kind of people were going to be going in. I had a feeling that it was a majority white church, but that really didn't bother me. Finally I decided to go in. I'm sure everyone reading this book has had experiences that you really can't put words on. And no matter how you try to articulate that experience, words simply don't do justice to it. It's something that has to be felt before it can be comprehended, and even then the experiences are somewhat different. This was one of those experiences. I don't know how to explain this, but the moment my foot crossed the threshold of that church, I knew it was the place I had been looking for all my life. My soul screamed with joy and delight. It was a true homecoming. Although I was the only black person in the church, I experienced unconditional love and acceptance like I had never received in any setting. Every face said, "You are welcome." I did everything I could to hold back the tears. The minister was wonderful. They also practice meditation (which I had begun to practice because of my exposure to eastern philosophy). That really confirmed for me that I was in the right place. My journey was over. I had found my church home. After the service, I received warm, loving hugs and smiles, and invitations for lunch. Initially I thought maybe they were just trying to solicit black membership, but that was definitely my own conversation. These people were expressing love the way God intended. I had found my heaven on earth.

I became completely committed to the Unity teachings and philosophies. I read all their literature and never missed a service. It was great. I started at the church in Friendswood, then I was forced to move to Austin, and continued my growth there. At the time I moved there, they were in transition with their minister. There was a new minister coming from another city. Some of the members seemed a little apprehensive at first, but the first day she spoke, I think she put everyone at ease. The first words out of her mouth when she took the podium were, "Let's get one thing straight, I'm no closer to God than you are, and I don't claim to have all the answers. But, I believe if we work together we can all grow and create some answers for all of us." I was instantly in love. She was exactly the type of teacher I needed to assist me in my spiritual growth. There were times when I would attend two services because I received so much from her messages. She is definitely one of Gods great messengers. After a little over a year, I moved back to Houston and started attending services there. After a few months I decided I wanted to talk to the minister. I made an appointment and went to his office.

As we sat there I informed him that I had never really trusted preachers. But since I had been attending Unity, my attitude had definitely changed. He smiled and welcomed me and told me that he understood. He told me that my relationship should be with God and not the minister, and I should make that first priority in my life. He promised if I did that, my life would work.

I left his office feeling really good. He was a great teacher, and the fact that he is a young minister makes it easier for me to listen to him. He never comes across with that holier-than-thou preacher mentality.

During this time a lot of things had not been going the way I planned. I had experienced several hardships (not having a car, and sometimes not even having a roof over my head). But I had decided to trust the Unity principles which teaches me that if I'm experiencing any pain or hardships there is a positive lesson in it somewhere if I'm willing to look deeply enough.

This philosophy definitely takes an incredible amount of faith. But if you adhere to it, I promise miracles do happen. The greatest miracle I've received since being a member of Unity is actually feeling the presence of God within me. After three and a half years of being a member and committing myself to God, I began to know that God was real. The miracles I received are far to numerous to put in this chapter, but I have to share my greatest miracle with you. As I mentioned earlier, it was easy for me to intellectualize the concepts and beliefs about being born again, but I had never really felt anything. Then one day, I came home from church after a powerful message. I didn't have a car at the time and I would ride my bike to church, which was approximately an hour away. While I was lying on my floor in my run down efficiency apartment with no furnishings except an airmattress, I started to thank God for the things that I did have. I had just purchased a copy of BeBe and CeCe Winans gospel tape *"Different Lifestyles,"* and I had a portable cassette player with headphones. As I lay on my airmattress and listened to the tape I started listening to a song titled "Searching for Love."

As I listened to the words, they were singing about searching for love, and he asked the question "Has any one found it?" He goes on to say that he found it, and it's more than just a feeling. It's the reality of the whole world. He goes on to say, "Love in the form of a babe that was born to reveal that love he was talking about." As I lay there listening to the song, I started to look back over the last few years of my life. I remembered my nice home, and family, my credit cards and nice secure job. Then I looked around at the bare walls of my apartment, and looked at my bicycle which was my only form of transportation. I had a total of sixteen dollars to my name and was over twenty thousand dollars in debt.

I continued to listen to the words, and all of a sudden something started happening in my gut. I kept listening to the words of the song and started thinking about my three year search for God. I started visualizing the message at church and I kept going back to where I used to be. All of a sudden that feeling that started in my gut reached my chest, then it felt as if my heart exploded with joy. And I realized I had found the love he was singing about. I realized that even though I didn't have all the material things that I had a few years ago, I had never been happier in my life. *I was experiencing life's ultimate paradox; to have absolutely nothing, yet have absolutely everything at the same time.* I had found God, and was feeling Him move through me. I cannot express the love and joy that came from within. I lay there on that mattress and cried for three hours straight. I kept listening to that song over and over again and it was as if God was speaking directly to me. For the first time, I was complete.

Although it had taken me over three years, I had found exactly what I was looking for and I had finally found the missing link in my life. I had confirmation that there really is a God.

My life hasn't been the same since. But now I don't just *believe in* God, I *know* God. There is a huge distinction between the two.

After that experience, I made the commitment to actually become a member of Unity Church. I finally found my church home, not in the building, but in my heart where God really lives.

I realize that everyone must ultimately make their own choice about God, and I would never say that what I believe is the only way. I would like to suggest that if you have experienced emptiness and pain in your life, drinking from the Spirit is definitely a solution.

The one thing I always hated about religion was the fact that people would try to force you to believe what they believed. This is probably why so many people shy away from religion. But I would like to suggest that there is a huge distinction to be made between religion and spirituality.

To me religion is what people do on Sundays. It's simply carrying the container without drinking what's in it. The reason I had such a big problem with Christianity was that "Christians" talked a good game, but they didn't walk their talk. It appeared to me that most Christians were really miserable and they practiced poverty as a virtue. I didn't want to have anything to do with that.

On the other hand, spirituality for me means recognizing God as my source, but understanding I am completely responsible for my actions. Unity teaches me that Christianity is a way of life, and if I choose to accept this way of life, then my actions have to be consistent with my beliefs. Instead of being labeled a "Christian," I simply need to follow the teachings of Jesus and my life works. That means drinking from the container and being grateful that my thirst has been quenched. Then I thank my creator, and He constantly keeps my container filled. I realize that I have an infinite supply of the divine thirst quencher, and my container can never be empty.

Spirituality for me means that every day is an opportunity for me to experience the joy of being alive. Creating an attitude of gratitude that says "Thanks God" for this wonderful gift called "life." Knowing that God has a purpose for me and, when I choose to accept that purpose, my life is a miracle.

In order for me to maintain my spirituality I have a three part system that keeps me grounded.

1. Prayer
2. Meditation
3. Contemplation

"Prayer" for me means talking to God. It doesn't mean I have to get on my knees, or use a bunch of religious mumbo jumbo. It simply means that I communicate with my mouth, my wants and needs to my Creator.

"Meditation" means listening to God. When I choose to listen, God will always provide me with the answers I need. It is that still small voice that directs me to my highest good.

"Contemplation" is thinking about God. When I marvel at the human anatomy, and see the beauty of creation, I'm thinking about God. When I reflect on my spiritual journey, and see how God was always there even when I chose not to accept him, I'm thinking about God.

I choose to incorporate these three elements into my life on a daily basis. Staying in contact with my source, is the way I keep my spiritual container filled.

If you choose to accept your spirituality, you will understand that although you follow the teachings of Jesus, you can also receive spiritual truth from other containers. It is my belief that we are currently moving towards a more spiritual way of life instead of religious. Although the negative approach towards God served it's purpose, we are entering into a time when we all operate out of positive spiritual truths. In John, Chapter 4:23, Jesus said "Yet a time is coming and now has come when the true worshipers will worship the father in spirit and truth, for they are the kind of worshipers the Father seeks. God is spirit, and his worshipers must worship in spirit and in truth."

To me that means just what I said. There are Universal Truths that include everyone and everything. When we choose to operate from love, then we express those truths. I realize that most fundamental religions put the majority of their focus on Jesus' death. But the truth is, His life is where we receive the real message. His entire teachings were about love and forgiveness, yet a lot of people focus on sin and punishment. Did you know that not once did Jesus ever call anyone a sinner? Never did he judge nor condemn. He of himself only gave one commandment and that was to "Love One Another". So if I choose Christianity as a way of life, then that's what I need to do, Love One Another. That's it, and that's that.

I definitely don't want to start preaching. I remember how that used to repulse me. I just want you to know that there is a God. You simply have to get thirsty enough to find him. No one can give it to you or find it for you.

Luke 11:9 states, "So I say unto you: Ask and it will be given to you; seek and you will find; knock and the door will be opened to you. For everyone who asks receives; he who seeks finds; and to him that knocks the door will be opened."

So, if you are ready to start knocking, get busy. Don't feel obligated to any container, try a few different ones until it feels right to you. If you really start looking, you will know when you've found the right one. Once you find one that's right for you, then get committed and participate. Take ownership of your relationship with your Creator. When you make it first priority in your life, everything else just falls into place.

I am definitely not saying that it's necessarily going to be easy. It took me three years to find what was right for me. But once you commit yourself to finding God, God will handle the rest.

But remember, "Seek ye first the kingdom of God and all things will be given unto you." I've probably heard that a million times. How about you? So where or what is this Kingdom Jesus kept talking about? If you will read Luke 17:20, Jesus said, "The kingdom of God does not come with your careful observation, nor will people say, 'Here it is' or 'There it is;' because the kingdom of God is within you." In Luke 9:27 Jesus says,"I tell you the truth, some who are standing here will not taste death before they see the kingdom of God."

What that says to me is that if I choose to find God in my heart (which I have) then I don't have to wait until I die before I enter the Kingdom. That means I can experience Heaven right here on earth, right now. (Which I do)

So the choice as always is yours.

I would like to close this chapter with the Unity prayer of protection. It has carried me through the roughest times of my life. If you could just know the truth in these words, you would never have to worry about anything again for the rest of your wonderful life. If you will recite these words to yourself on a daily basis you would immediately feel a shift in your spiritual being.

The Light Of God Surrounds Me.
The Love Of God Enfolds Me.
The Power Of God Protects Me.
The Presence Of God Watches Over Me.
Wherever I Am, God Is.
And All Is Well.
Thank You God!

Life moves on, whether we act as cowards or heroes
Life has no other discipline to impose,if we would
    but realize it than to accept life unquestioningly.
Everything we shut our eyes to, everything we run from,
    everything we deny, denigrate or despise,
    serves to defeat us in the end.
What seems nasty, painful, evil can become a source of beauty,
    joy and strength, if faced with an open mind.
Every moment is a golden one for him who has the vision to
recognize it as such.

HENRY MILLER

PURPOSE

Have you ever sat back and asked yourself "Why am I here?" That age old question of "What is the meaning of life?" Do you ever wonder if the purpose of our existence is to be born, live for eighty or ninety years (if we're lucky), then die. Of course you may have religious beliefs that say you have an opportunity to spend eternity in a gold paved heaven or a fire infested hell. But that's after the fact. I'm talking about the time right here on earth, right now. If you believe what the media tells us, it probably doesn't make a difference. It tells us that the world is a terrible place to be, and everybody is simply trying to take care of themselves. So we may as well wait for an afterlife and pray that it's better than this. Some people believe that they are actually going to be lifted up off the earth, then God is going to kill everybody else, then put them back so He can start all over with his chosen people. Hmmm. Well, you have probably noticed that I am the eternal optimist. And I say that all this negativity is a bunch of hogwash.

I believe that we should all be getting really excited because things are definitely going to get a lot better. Of course, these are my beliefs, so guess what? They have to show up in my experience. So let's go back to the original question. Why are you here?

I personally believe that each human being has a purpose. And if they are willing to find out what that purpose is, life is a joy. Unfortunately the vast majority of people never find out what their purpose is. In our society, we immortalize celebrities, sports heroes and, in some cases, businessmen. We put them up on these pedestals as though they were gods or something, and we somehow create a belief that they're different than other human beings. The truth is, they aren't. They're no different than you or me. They all have needs and feelings like everyone else, they all have to go to the bathroom like everybody else, and they even get diarrhea like everyone else. Of course, some of them do some pretty remarkable things, but the truth is, the only difference between them and us is their purpose.

"All men are created equal," is a very truthful statement. What separates men are the things that they accomplish. Just because a person makes a million dollars doesn't mean he's better than you; it simply means he has more money than you. But because of the way our society is set up, we think money is the gauge which we use to decide who's better than who. I suggest that you stop trying to go by society's standards, and decide to find your own purpose.

When we choose to take responsibility for our own destinies, life takes on a whole new meaning. We stop looking outside ourselves for answers.

I believe that we live in a perfect universe. Which means that there really is divine order in what appears to be total chaos. If we choose to find our purpose, then we become aligned with the universe and magic happens. No longer is our life stressful and full of emptiness and pain. But it becomes a joy, filled with happiness and abundance.

If my theory is correct, then all you need to do is get in alignment with your purpose and you can have anything you want in life.

If you really take some time to think about this, it really does make sense. For example, did you know that out of six billion people there is only one **you**. There never was and never will be another **you**. Why do you think we all have different fingerprints? The universe never duplicates itself. It automatically knows what it needs, and you were put here to do something that only you can do.

So how does one find his purpose?

First of all, I believe, that at the moment of our conception, God whispered in our hearts His purpose for us. It's been called "Our Hearts Desire" or "Our Dream." Whether you believe it or not, everyone has a dream. So if we accept this fact, it makes it easier for us to accept that maybe we do have a purpose.

So let's start at the beginning. Do you remember when you were a child and life was really magical? You could take a stick and turn it into a horse, or you could take an old box and turn it into a race car. During these times, we simply let our imaginations run free. In our minds we could be anyone or have anything we ever wanted. All we had to do was dream it and it was real. But as we became older, people around us started to convince us that we were silly to daydream and use our imagination. Our parents convinced us that we should start preparing to get nice steady responsible jobs; jobs that had prestige and paid well. We were taught to start thinking rationally and to only believe things that were rational and logical. Pretty soon we completely lost touch with our creativity and imagination.

Then before we knew it, we were caught in the "Drift." The drift is a metaphor for society. You see, most people float along this societal current of conformity and aren't even conscious of it. The Drift tells us that if we make a certain amount of money, then we will be happy. If we have a certain position within a large corporation, then we're successful. If we get married, buy a house, have 2.1 kids (where in the hell did they get that from) and a dog, then we are "Living the American Dream." So ultimately we buy into this. But the truth is, we've given up our dream and fallen victim to the Drift's dream. I have to admit, no one was more guilty of this than me. I was floating along the drift, doing everything it said, in order to be successful. I was floating aimlessly along that societal current, thinking that there was only one direction to go.

The truth is, once we accomplish the Drift's dream, we rationalize it by saying we're successful. Now we no longer have a need to dream, because we've made it. So, all we have to do now is sit back and wait for that societal safety valve called "retirement." In a way, society tricks us into giving up our dreams. What a shame! But there is good news! Remember what I said about the universe knowing what it needs. And obviously it knows it needs you or else you wouldn't be here. Right? Well, whether you realize it or not, the universe is constantly doing everything it can to remind you of your original dream.

Although you may be grown up and successful, how many times have you sat back and remembered the good times of being a kid. Maybe you loved baseball, and you have flash-

Purpose

backs of the times you played as a kid. Or maybe you love music, and you remember playing your air guitar and all of a sudden you feel really good inside. You forget about the everyday stresses and for a brief moment you are taken back to those magical moments of childhood. If you haven't done that in awhile, why not do it now? Think about some of those magical experiences you had as a child.

Did you dream of being an astronaut?
A Fireman?
A Businessman?
A Musician?
The first black billionaire?
An Artist?
An Actor?
A Pro Basketball or Football Player?

What were some of your dreams? Once you start remembering, notice what goes on inside. If you react to certain ones, you need to realize that the universe could be trying to remind you of your dream. Which in reality, is it's dream. It simply wants you to fulfill it. Please note: I use Universe interchangeably with God; to me they're one and the same.

So let's set up a scenario. Imagine you're floating along the Drift. As you're floating along, something keeps pulling at you. A part of you says, maybe you really don't want to be going in this direction. But then you look at everybody else and decide that you may as well continue since everybody else is. But there *is* something that keeps pulling at you; you ignore it. Then all of a sudden, you get stuck in the drift. Something within this current grabs you and won't let go. You keep fighting but it's got a firm hold on you.

Now the reason most people don't get out of the drift is because it's uncomfortable. Not only that, we're afraid what people will say about us. So why go against the flow? But every now and then, someone decides that they really don't want to go in the same direction as everybody else. They decide to stop. So what happens? People have to go around the obstruction, and they get angry and fuss and raise all sorts of hell. They try to force that person back into the flow. And usually, it works because we really don't want to cause too much trouble. Right? But if you choose to trust God, then you shouldn't worry about what other people think. Easier said than done.

Let's get back to you floating down the drift. This *thing* that keeps pulling on you is simply God trying to remind you of your dream. He is doing everything in his power to get your attention, but you continually ignore him. So He decides that He needs to take more drastic measures because He has something for you to do, and only you can do it.

Then He sends you what I label as a "Wake Up Call". In most cases a wake up call isn't a very pleasant experience. But it's usually the only way God can get our attention. As a matter of fact, I believe that we always have the opportunity to minimize the discomfort, if we would simply decide to listen.

My wake up call was my divorce. For the first time in my life, I had to really take a look at myself at a very deep level. I was caught in the drift and God kept telling me to grab His rope, but I wouldn't listen. As I look back, I realize I heard Him. I simply chose not to listen and it brought me an incredible amount of pain. But He knew His plan for me and He refused to let me drift aimlessly along the current. When I finally went on my journey to find Him, I realized how I had created a lot of unnecessary pain in my life. But as soon as I found Him, my whole life made sense. I could see how His plan for me was set in motion at a very early age. The dream in my youth of being my own boss was really His dream for me. And as long as I was working for that other company, then I could never live my dream. So I needed a wake up call, and, boy, I received one.

So in order to find your purpose, start at the beginning. Remember the things you loved doing as a child. Ask yourself what you really enjoy doing now? Does your current job allow you to express your creativity? Do you have any idea what being creative means? Some men think that only women are creative. NOT TRUE! We have a capacity for creativity just like women; we simply choose not to nurture it as much. Put a lot of thought into this. Notice the thoughts and feelings you have as you reflect on your childhood. A really good book to read on this subject is *DO IT! Let's get off our buts!* by John Rogers and Peter McWilliams. These guys are great!

After you've gotten back in touch with your dreams of childhood, start asking yourself when you decided to give up on your dreams. Ask yourself if you're caught in the drift. Then take a look at the current events in your life. Has the Universe been trying to tell you something, but you refuse to listen. Have you experienced any wake up calls lately? Are you constantly experiencing pain in your life, probably the same type of pain over and over again? Do you believe in a power greater than yourself? What are you willing to do to live your dreams.

I wrote this book to make you think. I wanted to interrupt your thought processes so that you could expose yourself to another way of thinking. Is it working?

Now that you have the basic fundamental structure of the drift and how the Universe works, let's do an exercise.

Take a moment and write down twenty things you dreamed of as a child. It doesn't matter what they are, just start writing. Remember that God gave you the idea very early; you simply forgot what it is. Writing things down will jog your memory. Once you've written them down, ask yourself if you attained any of them. Reflect on your life and see if you may still be heading towards your dream. Example: If you loved music as a child and you sing in a choir, chances are you're still headed for your dream. Now, ask yourself if you've had this feeling within that has been trying to tell you something. Have you been having daydreams about your dream? Have you been thinking about making a change in your life, but keep ignoring that *still small voice?* Is there something you've been dying to do, but you keep talking yourself out of it? Listen to that inner voice. If you're not sure what voice I'm talking about, it's the one that just said, "What voice is he talking about?"

It's up to you to find your own dream. You simply have to be willing to admit that you have one. As I mentioned, the reason we forget our dream is we choose to listen to other people instead of our own heart. Whenever I would tell people that one day I was going to be a millionaire, what do you think their response was? (Especially when you consider the circumstances that surrounded me.) What would you say to a young black male with only an eleventh grade education, if he walked up to you and said he was going to become a millionaire? You would probably tell him he'd better stay away from those drugs. Right? But I had a dream, and I simply became committed to it, and here I am. And if I can do it, you can to. All you need to do is believe that you can.

Have you ever noticed that the only requirement Jesus ever gave to accomplish anything was simply to believe that you could do it? He knew that God was the source working through him, so in reality His Dream was God's dream. That's why He never took credit for any miracle He ever accomplished. He would either say, "It is not I, but my father within that's doing His work." Or He would say, "Your faith has healed you." Not once did he say, "I did it." I apologize, I know I promised not to preach, but I felt it was relevant to guiding you to your dream.

Once you decide you have a dream, then what?

First, you need to recognize your Comfort Zones. You see, it's easy for anyone to have a great dream and never do anything about it. How many times have you listened to someone that really had a great idea, and even convinced you that their idea could work, yet they never took action?

The reason most people don't achieve their dreams is because in the process it can get pretty darn uncomfortable. And most of us simply don't like discomfort. So, what do we do? We develop comfort zones to keep us safe and comfortable. Then we rationalize by creating excuses to keep us from living our dreams. Of course, if you happen to be black, we've got the best built in rationalization there is: The White Man. Using the white man as an excuse not to live our dreams is a comfort zone. It is simply a rationalization we can use to keep from getting uncomfortable. If we decide that our dream is to own our own company, and after a few rejections we don't receive funding, we can always blame it on the white man or racism. The end result: no dream. Then we fail to take responsibility, and place the blame on something outside of ourselves. I realize that makes a lot of people angry but we have to understand that we have the power to do anything we want if we choose to. So we can no longer make excuses for not living our dream.

So, you have to decide what your comfort zones are. For example: If you are uncomfortable around white people, you need to ask why? Then you need to be around as many white people as you can, until you are comfortable. Because if you plan on living your dreams, I promise you will have to deal with them. (As I mentioned, you should try to get into the habit of not having that conversation.) The point is, if you are uncomfortable in this situation, chances are you will rationalize this as racism, and stay within your comfort zone. Then you will become immobilized.

The thing to remember about the comfort zone is you should always be expanding it.

Remember CANI™. All CANI™ means is expanding your comfort zone. It may be uncomfortable at first, but the more you stretch, the easier it gets.

So take a moment and list some of your comfort zones. Make a list of ten situations that make you uncomfortable. This is essential. If you aren't aware of your comfort zones you will continually avoid them unconsciously. And they will sabotage your dreams.

Here's a few things to consider:

1. Are you uncomfortable around white people?
2. If you don't have a college degree, are you uncomfortable around people that do?
3. Do you get nervous around authority figures?
4. Are you uncomfortable around other genders? How do you feel about being in a room filled with members of the opposite sex.
5. Are you able to receive direct compliments?

As you think about these situations, notice any feelings you may have. This takes rigorous honesty on your part. You need to be completely honest with yourself. Once you have identified your comfort zones you have to be willing to "Feel the Fear and Do It Anyway." This is what separates the men from the boys! If you commit yourself to facing your fears, you gain personal power. As long as you run away from your fears, you give your power to the circumstance, and you will never live your dreams that way.

You have to be willing to confront the fear first, then it will go away. So make a habit of expanding your comfort zone, and you can live your dreams.

I would like to share a universal truth that may make things a little easier to understand. It is a universal law that was put in motion by the Creator himself. I call it: "The Breakdown-Breakthrough Principle!"

If you look throughout nature, there is an incredible process of life. For example: when you plant a seed, it has to go through what I call the Breakdown Period. Which is the time it takes for the seed to develop roots and a secure foundation. This period is essential to its growth. It provides the plant with the strength to withstand all the adversities it will experience once it breaks through the surface of the ground. Once the root system or foundation is developed, then it breaks the ground and grows to become a beautiful expression called a flower or a tree depending on the seed. Once it expresses this, then it's in the Breakthrough Period. It is the period that we usually put the most emphasis on. When was the last time you heard someone say, "What a beautiful root system that rose has?" We see the beauty of the rose yet we neglect to acknowledge that the rose couldn't exist without its roots. Of course we should acknowledge the beauty of the rose, but when we understand the process, it simply makes the rose more beautiful.

The point is, you are just like the rose. When you choose to live your dreams, you understand that you are the seed that God has planted, and the Breakdown Periods you experience are simply His way of making sure your roots are firmly planted in spiritual soil. Once your

Purpose

roots are steadfast, then God will allow you to express all the splendor within you.

So as you're chasing your dreams and everything seems to be going wrong, just remember, God is with you and there is a reason for your discomfort. Affirm to yourself. "I realize I am in major Breakdown right now but I know God is with me and preparing me for His Breakthrough and all is well." This may sound simplistic, but if you knew that were true, would you have a reason to be worried? You simply have to believe! That's all.

So now you understand the Drift, you know how God plants you as a seed to express all that He is, and you realize that you've got to commit yourself to expanding your comfort zone on a regular basis. You realize that any discomfort you experience holds a valuable lesson for your growth, and you've got your Breakdown Breakthrough prayer imbedded in your consciousness. You know you have a purpose and you are now chasing your dream. So I would now like to share with you the five key words to live your dreams. Put these words to memory, and go over them on a daily basis. These five words hold the keys to your success and purpose.

1. VISION.

The reason most people don't live their dreams is simply because they have no idea what their dreams are. Make sure you have a clear vision of your dream. It needs to be specific and quantifiable. Remember your childhood list. Find your dream then put it on paper. Remember that it's really God's dream anyway, he simply needs you to do it for Him. Visualize yourself accomplishing your dreams and assume the same feelings you would have as if you had already lived your dream. If you accomplish one dream, don't stop there, accomplish another one. Keep growing and keep expanding.

2. COMMITMENT

Next to love, this is the second most powerful force in the universe. It works hand in hand with faith. When you make a commitment to something it tells the universe that you are really serious about your dream. Then the universe says, "Okay, let's get busy." There is no such thing as being half committed. Either you are or you aren't. The one way to quantify this is by your result. If you are completely committed your results will show. If you don't have the desired result, you simply weren't committed. There are no if's, and's ,or buts about it. So get committed and create your dream.

3. PASSION

You've got to have Passion to live your dream. Another word for passion is enthusiasm, which means energy of the divine. Once you get passion nothing can hold you back. It is simply God within trying to express through you. How many times have you watched an activist of some type chain themselves to fences or lay down in front of cars because they believed in something. You may disagree with what they are doing, but there is no denying that they are Passionate about what they believe in. Dr. Martin Luther King Jr. said: "To have lived and not believed in something you would have died for, is to not have lived at all." You've got to have passion! Now ask yourself this question: "Is it possible to be passionate about something you hate?" I don't think so. That's why you have to find your dream because when you do, I promise you will definitely be passionate about it. If you are currently involved in a job you hate I can promise you, you have no passion about it, and you and your employer both lose. Whatever you do, do it with passion.

4. PERSEVERANCE

Winston Churchill said "Never, never, never, never quit!" I say these are words to live by. Most people get extremely close, then give up at the very last moment. I would like to share a poem with you that really says this better than I can:

When things go wrong, as they sometimes will,
When the road you're trudging seems all uphill,
When the funds are low and the debts are high,
And you want to smile, but you have to sigh,
When care is pressing you down a bit,
Rest, if you must but don't you quit.
Life is queer with its twist and turns,
As everyone of us sometimes learns.
And many a failure turns about,
When they might have won had they stuck it out.
Don't give up, though the pace is slow
You may succeed with another blow.
Often the struggler has given up
When they might have captured the victors cup.
And they learned too late, when the height slipped down.
How close they were to the golden crown.
Success is failure turned inside out.
The silver tint of the clouds of doubt.
And you can never tell how close you are.
It may be near when it seems afar.
So stick to the fight when your hardest hit-
It's when things seem worst that you mustn't quit.

Author Unknown
(That's perseverance!)

5. GRATITUDE

This word is as important, if not more important, than any of the other four. This is the word that a lot of people leave out and then they wonder why they aren't enjoying their success. If we understand that God is the source of our good, then we need to thank Him for that good. When we learn to be grateful for whatever we have at the present moment, God will bless us with more. It is the attitude of gratitude that creates deep joy within our hearts. If you can acknowledge God during rough times, then you definitely need to acknowledge Him during good times. I have a prayer that I use that goes like this:

"Dear God I surrender everything to you. I give you my health, my relationships, my finances and my life. I thank you for the opportunity to be in your service and my only request is that you keep me from getting a big head. Thank you."

It's really a prayer of gratitude, and it gives me incredible serenity and peace. If you really want to experience a deep level of joy, you might want to try making a list of twenty-five things you have to be grateful for. Write the list right before you go to bed, and do it for one week. I promise you will have a new way to look at life. And I promise God will send you more things to be grateful for. The reason a lot of people are so miserable is because they always focus on what's wrong instead of what's right. Therefore they will always create whatever they focus on. Be grateful!

So let's summarize the five key words to live your dreams.
1. Vision
2. Commitment
3. Passion
4. Perseverance
5. Gratitude.

Follow the steps in this chapter and there is nothing you can't accomplish.

And Remember:
The world moves aside
to let any man pass
if he knows where he is going!

To laugh often and much;
to win the respect of intelligent people
    and the affection of children;
to earn the appreciation of honest critics and endure
    the betrayal of false friends.
to appreciate beauty;
to find the best in others;
to leave the world a bit better,
    whether by a healthy child,
        a garden patch or a redeemed social condition;
to know even one life has breathed easier because
    you haved lived.
This is to have succeeded.

                                        EMERSON

SERVICE

Without question, God's greatest creation is the human body. Jesus said "Tear down the temple of God and I will rebuild it in three days!" The temple he spoke of was his physical body. It is my belief that the human body is simply a microcosm of the universe. 1st Corinthians 12:14 through 12:27 states:

"Now the body is not made up of one part but of many. If the foot should say, 'Because I am not a hand, I do not belong to the body,' it would not for that reason cease to be part of the body. And if the ear should say, 'Because I am not an eye, I do not belong to the body,' it would not for that reason cease to be part of the body. If the whole body were an eye, where would the sense of hearing be? If the whole body were an ear, where would the sense of smell be? But, in fact, God has arranged the parts in the body, every one of them, just as he wanted them to be. If they were all one part, where would the body be? As it is, there are many parts, but one body. The eye cannot say to the hand, "I don't need you!" And the head cannot say to the feet, "I don't need you!" On the contrary, those parts that seem to be weaker are indispensable, and the parts that we think are less honorable, we treat with special honor. And the parts that are unpresentable, are treated with special modesty, while our presentable parts need no special treatment. But God has combined the members of the body, and has given great honor to the parts that lacked it, so that there should be no division in the body, but it's parts should have equal concern for each other. If one part suffers, every part suffers with it: if one part is honored, every part rejoices with it. Now you are the body of Christ, and each one of you is a part of it."
I believe this passage substantiates my belief.

Take a moment and think about your body. It is definitely the greatest miracle in the world. Think about how your organs are perfectly placed within. Your heart, lungs, kidneys, intestines, spleen, gall bladder and of course your brain are all strategically placed within the framework of God's greatest creation.

If you cut yourself, the cells within automatically know what has to take place in order to heal the wound. You don't have to think to yourself, "Cells, I need you to fix this cut." The cells do this automatically. When a person exercises, the muscles automatically know that they have to grow in order to compensate for the extra strength needed to lift the weights. The harder you work the human body, the stronger it becomes. Have you ever really thought about the miracle healing power of the human body? If you break a bone, how does it heal? Some people think, "I go to a doctor, they put a cast on it and it's healed." That is true, but we need to take a closer look at the process. As I've mentioned, the internal cells automatically know what has to take place in order for the healing to occur. But how do the cells know this?

Obviously there is some divine intelligence within the cells that direct them to do their particular duty. This divine intelligence, I believe, is God.

It is that life giving energy within the cells of every living creature that automatically knows what has to happen in order to heal a living organism.

Now take a moment and think about the earth. Imagine that the earth is just like your body. It has strategically placed organs which we call countries and millions of cells which we call people. Like your body it is sometimes invaded by germs and diseases. Some of the diseases that attack the earth body are: Wars, Hatred, Racism and Fear. Think back to the Persian Gulf war. Think of Kuwait as a kidney within the earth body. The kidney was invaded by a germ called Saddam Hussein. This germ tried to take over the entire organ. As it made its initial attempt at taking over the organ, several other cells decided to be like the germ and started acting like it. Now we have a disease because the germ has started to multiply.

But because of the divine intelligence of the whole body, it had to start healing itself by sending out some good cells to get rid of the bad germs. So enter in the U.S. military. The military acted as the good cells within the earth body and started the process of healing. I personally never condone wars, I simply wanted to use this analogy to let you see the big picture. The point is, you are a cell within the body of God. Like a cell within the human body you have a specific purpose. That purpose is to heal the body.

Although the media would have you believe that the world is in total chaos, I would like to assert to you, at this time, that what is actually taking place is God's body is actually healing itself. I also believe that this healing process has begun to accelerate and, as we move towards the next millennium, we will experience a new level of peace and understanding. If you will take a moment and think about the world events that are now taking place, you should be able to see what I'm talking about. For example: think back only ten years ago and ask yourself what was our belief about Russians? As Americans, the majority of us thought they were all commie bastards, full of hatred and ignorance, and, of course, we could never trust them. Now we've got them on our basketball teams! If you think about the eternality of time, ten years is just a blink of an eye. Never in the history of the world have we been closer to world peace than we are right now. Take a look at all the military cutbacks and base closings that are taking place right now. This is a positive sign of what to expect in the future. Remember the Divine Intelligence; it knows what it needs to heal itself. It doesn't have to think about it. It simply happens.

As a single cell in the body of God, when you choose to assist in healing the body, then you are in service. As I've mentioned, that is the reason for our existence. To serve. Whenever you hear someone talk about the will of God, it simply means that you are doing your part in healing the body.

Another word for that divine healing power is Love. It is simply God in action directing you to your highest good to assist Him in healing His body. When a human being chooses to spread love unconditionally, he becomes the antidote for all illnesses. When we drink from that fountain of Love and spread that Love around, the body becomes filled with Love and

Service

ultimately becomes healed.

All throughout history God has given certain cells the task of healing his body on a very large scale. It is my belief that Jesus was the ultimate healer. He tapped into that infinite well of Love and created a healing process that transcended all other great healing masters. Jesus was the ultimate cell in the body of God. But as He mentioned in John 14:12 "I tell you the truth, anyone who has faith in me will do what I have been doing. He will do even greater things than these, because I am going to the Father. And I will do whatever you ask in my name, so that the son may bring glory to the Father."

That means that we all have the capacity to heal just like He did. All we need to do is make a conscious effort to follow His teachings and the world will be healed. Most of us don't believe that we have that same power. I think it frightens us to think that we could actually do the things that Jesus did. But the truth is, we all have a voice to speak out in truth, and each one of us can contribute to the healing process. When I think about Dr. Martin Luther King Jr., I realize that he also tapped into that infinite well of love. Because of his commitment to non-violence he showed us that with love he could move mountains. And he did. Rather than accept all the anger and hatred that surrounded him on a daily basis, he chose to follow his heart and surrender to God. He followed Jesus' lead to not try and defuse anger with anger, but with love. I realize a lot of people still believe that we should fight fire with fire and retaliate with anger and hatred, but that only creates more of the same. Hatred and anger creates disease within the body of God and it only slows the healing process.

To assist in this process we must first take an honest look at ourselves and see how we are participating in life at this particular moment. If you have read through this book, you may have noticed some areas in which you can make some changes within yourself that will assist in the healing of the planet. In order to heal, a cell must be healthy first. If it is contaminated, then it will only spread that contamination. Once you have become healthy, then start spreading yourself around to assist other people in becoming healthy. As I mentioned, each human being is created the same. They simply have a different purpose. So never try and compare yourself to other people, simply be the best that you can be in all areas of your life. I promise you will be automatically doing your part in healing the planet.

If you are looking for some specific ways in which to assist in the healing of the planet, let me make a few suggestions.

First and foremost, **learn to love yourself**. I realize that may come as a shock to some of you, but that is the key. Four years ago, if someone even mentioned the word love, I became uncomfortable and would accuse that person (if they were male) of being weak and overly sensitive. But if you ever experience true love on a deep, emotional, spiritual level the way I have over the last year, you would definitely have a change of heart. You would also know what it feels like to experience heaven right here on earth.

Taking the time to understand ourselves first is the key to being happy.

Next, I believe that a spiritual connection of some sort is essential. Remember, it doesn't matter what container you're drinking from, just make sure you're getting your spiritual thirst quenched. You have to make sure that you are tapping into that well on a daily basis. This is an absolute must. The more you drink the more you get. Make sure that you are participating in something that uplifts you spiritually, not something that drags you down with guilt and negativity. If there is a Unity Church of Christianity in your area, you might consider giving it a try. Whatever you choose, make sure it makes you feel good. That's the difference between religion and spirituality. Spirituality feels great because you are tapping into that life giving force of love. In some cases, religion is extremely uncomfortable because it pushes shame and condemnation on you, and that goes against the true nature of who you are.

Give something back! We each have special gifts and talents that we should use to be in service to our Creator. Acknowledge those gifts and share them with someone. Whenever you're being creative, you're simply letting that infinite intelligence flow through you. If you love to sing, then start singing, If you love to dance, start dancing. Whatever you choose to do, do it with love and passion. Remember when you were a kid and you weren't concerned about what people thought of you and you would sing or dance at a moments notice? You were simply expressing yourself, and it felt great. If you will simply be yourself and love what you do, then you are being in service. For example, writing this book is a way of being in service. It allows me to not only share my experiences with you, but hopefully empower you to take action and heal the planet. You don't have to write a book to give something back, although I do suggest that you consider it. By sharing our positive uplifting stories, we empower others to share their stories. As soon as we start focusing on what's right instead of what's wrong, we will start creating more things that are right. Giving back means spreading love. You can do that by smiling at a stranger or helping someone with a flat tire. You can donate a pint of blood or volunteer your services. Have you ever noticed how good it feels to give love unconditionally. Whenever you do that you are simply expressing God. Maybe you're walking down the street and you give a homeless person a dollar without any thoughts of getting something in return. All of a sudden something inside says, "Way to go!" My favorite is hugs, of course most men are extremely uncomfortable with this, but I love them. Especially from my kids. When was the last time you had a great hug? If more people hugged each other, we could melt away a lot of pain.

Make a commitment to love yourself and others, and do everything with love. When you do this you, will experience Heaven on Earth the way God intended. **Commit yourself to service.**

I hope this book has provided some information and inspiration to assist you in being all you were created to be. You have to believe that you do have the power within you to live your dreams and enjoy a life filled with joy peace and love. I realize some of you reading this may still be rationalizing in your head how "Unmanly" loving yourself and the planet is, but I used to do the same thing. It was that masculine conversation that almost cost me my life. I sincerely hope that you will not make the same mistakes I did. Whether you admit it or not, at

Service

the core of your being is love. You can choose to accept this or you can continue to experience pain and emptiness in your life. I promise that the love and joy beats out the pain and sorrow any day. You don't have to pretend any longer, all you have to do is take action. Make a commitment to love yourself, and you will be doing your part in healing the world.

So I would like to summarize by going back over the chapters and their significance.

First, we must recognize any limiting beliefs we have about ourselves or others. We have to accept the fact that each culture has their own beliefs, and though they may be different from yours, it doesn't make them any better or worse.

Next we must commit ourselves to CANI™ (Constant And Never-ending Improvement.) Never stop learning. Always realize that the road of life has no destination. It's simply a magical journey with no end.

We must create, open, loving, caring intimate relationships with ourselves and others. We need to understand that, as human beings, we are all intimately connected with each other. And if there is pain amongst one of us, there is pain amongst all of us.

We must destroy society's delusion of sexual encounters. We have to recognize that sexual conquest are not a gauge for manhood. We have to commit ourselves to making love to our mates not just having sex with them.

We must love and cherish our children. This has to be top priority. We cannot abuse our children in any way, verbal, physical or otherwise. We must take time to develop close, supportive relationships with our children.

We must take care of our physical bodies. I believe that a minimum of seventy-five percent of our deaths and illnesses are preventable. That means exercise and moderation of food consumption. We must remove drug and alcohol addiction from our society.

We must have careers that are rewarding and fulfilling; doing what we love and being compensated accordingly.

We must maintain a spiritual foundation. We must tap into that divine part of us that is God, our true selves.

We must recognize our own individual gifts and talents. We must eliminate this male competitiveness that causes us to constantly try and outdo other men. When we express who we are with love, there will always be room for each individual. We have to empower each other to express their gifts.

And finally, we must commit ourselves to be in service; healing the body of God by loving ourselves and others. Then and only then can we experience Heaven on Earth.

If we choose to take responsibility for ourselves, everything else will fall into place. If we all follow these guidelines, the world will be just as God planned it. I hope you choose to do your part. I have!

I LOVE YOU & GOD BLESS YOU
Michael

If you would like to have Michael speak at your organization or would simply like to comment on *Brothers, Are You Listening?*, please forward your correspondence to:

Creation Publishing Group
6355 Westheimer #187
Houston, Texas 77057

To order a copy or copies of *Brothers, Are You Listening?*, simply fill out the order form below.

CREATION PUBLISHING GROUP™
6355 Westhelmer #187, Houston, Texas 77057
Phone: (713) 267-0600   Fax: (713) 975-1114

Ship to: _____

Name: _____

Address: _____

City, State, Zip: _____

Phone: _____

Fax: _____
❑ Check this box if you have special instructions on back of this form

BROTHERS, ARE YOU LISTENING? is just $15.95
plus $5.00 shipping & handling per book.

I would like _____ copy(s) of "BROTHERS, ARE YOU LISTENING?"

Total $ amount including shipping _____

Orders will be shipped UPS to a street address only. (Not a P.O. Box)
Tax is included in the prices listed.

CREATION PUBLISHING GROUP™